**To my son and grandson, Antonin & Gabin,
so that they never forget their roots.
Con amore,
Vostra nonna**

                                                Enza

ENZA GENOVESE

SICILY

RECIPES FROM AN ITALIAN ISLAND

MITCHELL BEAZLEY

Contents

Sicilian family recipes ... 4
Sicilian cuisine ... 8

Appetizers 13
Aubergine cream with anchovies ... 14
Salt cod and olive fritters ... 16
A word on antipasti ... 18
Potato croquettes ... 20
Small 'fritter' pizzas ... 22
Arancini ... 24
Chickpea pancake ... 29
Sicilian chickpea fritters ... 29
Sicilian pizza 'rianella' ... 30
Sicilian focaccia ... 32
Sweet-and-sour pumpkin ... 36
Aubergine caponata ... 39
Caponata pie ... 40
Chard and fennel pie ... 44
Nonna's stuffed aubergines ... 46
Seafood salad ... 50
Sicilian parmigiana ... 52

Pasta 55
Penne with pistachios and bottarga ... 56
Bucatini with sardines ... 58
Casarecce with aubergines and ricotta salata ... 62
Oven-baked pasta ... 64
Busiate with Trapani pesto ... 67
Fusilli with Aeolian Island pesto ... 67
A word on pasta ... 70
Spaghetti with ricotta and pistachios ... 72
Sicilian cannelloni ... 76
Sea urchin roe and artichoke linguine ... 78
Ricotta-filled ravioli ... 84

Risottos and couscous 87
Fisherman's risotto ... 88
Grilled octopus and ginger risotto ... 92

A word on risottos and couscous	94
Lobster risotto	96
Artichoke and pea risotto	100
Trapani couscous	102
Couscous with cuttlefish, mussels and prawns	106

Meat — 109

Small meat pies	110
Meatloaf with vegetable sauce	114
Nonna's glazed meat and egg roll	116
Pork stew	120
Meatballs au naturel	122
Veal escalopes and ham served pizza-style	126

Fish — 129

Oven-baked turbot with bottarga	130
Braised salt cod	132
Sweet-and-sour sea bass carpaccio	134
Beer-battered salt cod	138
Tuna carpaccio	140
Sardine tartlets	144
Hearty octopus soup	146
Stuffed squid	148
Swordfish with capers and almonds	152
Mackerel with orange pesto	154

Desserts — 157

Sicilian cannoli	158
Cassatelle	162
Ricotta tart	164
Doughnuts	168
Sicilian cassata	172
Nonna Lucia's sweet fritters	174
A word on desserts	178
Soft almond biscuits	180
Blancmange	182
Fig biscuits	186
Arancini with chocolate cream	188
Index	190
Acknowledgements	191
UK/US terms	192

Sicilian family recipes

WELCOME TO OUR HOME AND BUON APPETITO!

My Sicilian family arrived in southern France, or more precisely in Montpellier, in 1961. I can recall seeing my parents experiencing both sadness and excitement as they embarked on their new lives. They soon took over a former grocery shop in Montpellier's historic centre, close to the great Halles Castellane and the Place Jean-Jaurès. They wanted to sell Italian produce – spices, olives, different olive oils, coffee, dried vegetables and much besides... a way of maintaining their links with Sicily. Their shop was a veritable Aladdin's cave, full of colours and aromas, and a warm, welcoming place. Customers enjoyed meeting there and discussing and sharing recipes. I revelled in this atmosphere and, from the age of five, food became my passion.

Each summer we would drive the entire length of Italy to visit some of our family back in Sicily. As soon as we had settled in, we loved to get up early to go to the market in Trapani, a city on the west coast, not just for the fresh fruit and vegetables from the surrounding countryside, but to watch the fishing boats bring different kinds of fresh fish into the port. We'd see huge groupers, ideal for making fish couscous, swordfish for barbecuing and, of course, the legendary tuna, an unmissable speciality in this western region. Sicilian cooks use every part of the tuna, the most valuable being the roe sac to make salted, cured bottarga, but also *ventresca* (the oil-rich belly fillet), which is preserved in olive oil, and *carubella*, a spicy sausage that is eaten on Sicilian bread made with semolina and sesame seeds. Another speciality lodged in my memory is the *brioche con panna e gelsomino* that we enjoyed once the market was over. The brioches were filled with jasmine ice cream and topped with whipped cream – we ate them before returning home where the rest of the family had been busy since early morning making fresh pasta for lunch. I carefully recorded all these recipes and memories in my notebook, which has become an enduring link with our traditions and roots.

Over the years, my parents' shop filled up with new Italian products, including *salumi* (cold cured meats), homemade pasta, cheeses (especially large wheels of Parmesan), tomato sauces, sweet breads, such as panettone at Christmastime, and many more. The passion for Italy and its delicious produce has never left me and, naturally, I took over the grocery when my parents retired.

Since then, my husband and I have never stopped travelling all over Italy and, of course, Sicily, in search of new producers and products. I wanted to pass on to my children the story of my origins through the universal language of a mother's cooking, so I dedicated my first manuscript exclusively to them. Today, I'm dedicating this book to the customers of the shop and my loyal friends who have accompanied me on this family adventure. I remember and hold in my heart all the good times I have shared with them. The book is also dedicated to everyone who loves Sicily.

My thanks to all of you.

Enza Genovese

SICILIAN cuisine

Sicily is an incredibly diverse land, not only in terms of its natural and artistic beauty but also its traditions, which vary from city to city and from village to village. For several centuries, the island was ruled by different populations: Roman, Greek, Byzantine, Arab, Norman, Spanish and many others. Each, in its own way, has influenced Sicilian cuisine, making it a rich, complex and varied gastronomy.

In this book, I have brought together Sicilian recipes, not simply to explore the flavours of a simple and generous cuisine but also to celebrate the produce of both land and sea. That wealth of food includes fish and seafood, extra-virgin olive oil, garlic, olives, capers, lemons and oranges, abundant herbs, fennel, pine nuts, raisins, almonds, hazelnuts, pistachios, ancient wheat pasta, spelt, couscous, vegetables, cheeses (caciocavallo, pecorino), desserts made with candied fruits, sheep's milk ricotta, honey, chocolate, sponge cake, ice cream and granita. And, of course, we cannot overlook Sicily's strong winemaking tradition, with its 28 indigenous grape varieties, 23 wine regions awarded DOC (Designation of Origin Controlled) status, and one granted the highest-quality designation, DOCG (Designation of Origin Controlled and Guaranteed). For some dishes, I have suggested a Sicilian wine that will perfectly complement your meal.

So, join me and discover all this wonderful produce through my family's recipes. Above all, never forget that the secret of making a good dish is to start with the finest ingredients!

Appetizers

ANTIPASTI

Aubergine cream with anchovies
Crema di melanzane con le acciughe

This cream forms part of what we call *stuzzichini*, small appetizers designed to tempt your tastebuds before the main meal. The Sicilian aubergine is distinguished by its round shape and light purple colour, and it has very few seeds. Mild in flavour, combining it with garlic and anchovies allows it to develop real character!

Preparation time: 15 minutes
Draining time: 1 hour
Cooking time: 1 hour
Serves 4

- 1kg (2lb 4oz) round Sicilian Violette aubergines or long aubergines, washed and halved lengthways
- 4 anchovies preserved in salt, or 80g (2¾oz) canned anchovies in olive oil
- 2 garlic cloves, chopped
- 4 tablespoons olive oil
- 4 tablespoons white wine vinegar
- 2 tablespoons lemon juice
- slices of sourdough, toasted
- salt (fine and coarse) and freshly ground black pepper

Lightly sprinkle the cut sides of the aubergines with coarse salt and place on a rack for 1 hour to draw out their bitterness. Preheat the oven to 200°C (400°F), Gas Mark 6.

Rinse the aubergines, wipe dry with kitchen paper, then wrap in foil and bake for 1 hour. Remove from the oven, unwrap and leave to cool. Using a spoon, scoop out the aubergine flesh into a bowl.

Remove the bones from the anchovies, rinse if using those preserved in salt, and crush them or leave in small pieces. Mix the anchovies and garlic with the aubergine flesh, season with a pinch of fine salt and freshly ground black pepper, then add the olive oil, a little at a time, stirring constantly. Add the vinegar and lemon juice and mix until the ingredients are thoroughly combined. Chill in the refrigerator until ready to serve.

Spread the aubergine cream on toasted sourdough and serve as an accompaniment to aperitifs.

Tip

Serve with a Marsala Cremovo (see page 172) or Marsala Fine semisecco. Marsala is a quintessential aperitif wine in Sicily (best served chilled). The sweetness of the wine beautifully balances the anchovy and garlic flavours in this dish.

Salt cod and olive fritters
Frittelle di baccalà alle olive

Salt cod is a staple in many Mediterranean countries and regularly features on Sicilian tables. It is frequently eaten on Fridays but, more especially, to celebrate religious festivals. Deep-frying it as fritters makes it even tastier, of course!

Preparation time: 25 minutes
Soaking time: 20 minutes
Cooking time: 30–40 minutes
Serves 4

- 10g (¼oz) salted capers
- bunch of flat-leaf parsley
- 30g (1oz) pine nuts
- 9 tablespoons olive oil
- 500g (1lb 2oz) salt cod, desalted (see Tip) and cut into pieces
- 200g (7oz) potatoes
- 1 egg, beaten
- finely grated zest of ½ unwaxed lemon
- 30g (1oz) Taggiasche olives, pitted and chopped
- 80g (2¾oz) leek, white part only, finely chopped
- 100g (3½oz) dry breadcrumbs
- oil, for deep-frying
- salt and freshly ground black pepper

Rinse the capers, soak them in cold water for 20 minutes, then drain. Put half of the capers, three-quarters of the parsley, the pine nuts, 7 tablespoons of the olive oil, a pinch of salt, some freshly ground pepper and 3–4 tablespoons of cold water into a liquidizer or food processor. Blend to make a smooth parsley pesto, adding a little more water, if necessary, then set aside.

Rinse the desalted salt cod pieces (see Tip below), place in a saucepan, cover with cold water and bring to the boil, then simmer for about 10 minutes. Drain the salt cod, remove the skin and any bones, then, using your hands, flake the flesh into a bowl.

Boil the potatoes in a saucepan of salted water until tender. Drain and mash, then add to the salt cod. Mix in the egg, the remaining parsley, the lemon zest, olives and the rest of the capers.

Heat the remaining 2 tablespoons of olive oil with a pinch of salt and 50ml (2fl oz) of water in a saucepan and sweat the leek over a medium heat for 5 minutes until the water has evaporated. Stir the leek into the potatoes and salt cod. Shape the mixture into small balls and roll them in the breadcrumbs until they are evenly coated.

Heat enough oil for deep-frying in a deep-sided saucepan to 180–190°C (350–375°F), or until a cube of bread browns in 30 seconds. Fry the fritters, in batches if required, until they are golden brown all over. Drain on a plate lined with kitchen paper and serve with aperitifs, accompanied with the parsley pesto for dipping.

Tip

To desalt salt cod, simply soak in cold water for 2–3 days, changing the water 3–4 times a day.

Serve with a St Germain brut spumante or another sparkling wine of your choice.

A word on antipasti

In Sicily, and throughout Italy, a meal starts with antipasto, which translates as 'before the main dish'. Traditional Sicilian cuisine has many mouthwatering appetizers and it is customary to serve an array of *stuzzichini* (pre-dinner nibbles). These could be large green olives *cunzate* (marinated with a mixture of chopped garlic, celery and other vegetables and seasoned with dried oregano and wine vinegar). There are also the famous *cucunci*, caper berries on stalks, Ragusano pecorino cheese accompanied by fresh broad beans, tiny pizzas, potato croquettes, fritters made with chickpea flour, arancini… and much more. All of them are accompanied with a fine glass of Marsala, Malvasia delle Lipari, muscat or Zibibbo di Pantelleria (also known as Muscat of Alexandria). And, for those who don't drink alcohol, a delicious and refreshing lemonade or sparkling orange soda will do nicely!

I've so far forgotten to mention that Sicilian mothers always, as a matter of course, prepare too much food to ensure there is enough for the unexpected guest. A famous Sicilian proverb perfectly sums this up: 'The guest does not come in by the front door, but by the one that is open.' And they always leave with a small parcel of food…

Potato croquettes
Crocchette di patate

These croquettes can form part of a selection of *stuzzichini* (pre-dinner nibbles) and are also sold as street food. This is the basic recipe, but they will be even more satisfying if you stuff them with small cubes of smoked scamorza cheese.

Preparation time: 25 minutes
Cooking time: 30–40 minutes
Makes 25–30 croquettes

- 1kg (2lb 4oz) small, red potatoes, preferably La Ratte or Roseval, unpeeled and scrubbed
- 2 egg yolks, plus 1 whole egg
- 12 flat-leaf parsley sprigs, very finely chopped, or 3 tablespoons chopped parsley
- 100g (3½oz) grated Parmesan cheese
- 100g (3½oz) dry breadcrumbs
- oil, for deep-frying
- 1 teaspoon salt
- black pepper
- lemon slices, to garnish

Boil the potatoes in a saucepan of salted water for about 30 minutes, or until tender. Drain and, when cool enough to handle, peel off the skins and mash the potatoes in a large bowl.

Beat the 2 egg yolks with the salt, black pepper and chopped parsley. Add to the mashed potatoes along with the grated Parmesan and mix well. Using your hands, shape the mixture into rolls about 6cm (2½in) long and 2cm (¾in) wide, and place them on a sheet of nonstick baking paper. You should be able to make about 30.

Heat enough oil for deep-frying in a large, deep-sided saucepan to 180–190°C (350–375°F), or until a cube of bread browns in 30 seconds.

Beat the whole egg in a shallow dish and spread the breadcrumbs over a large plate. Coat the croquettes first in beaten egg then in breadcrumbs until evenly coated. Deep-fry the croquettes, in two batches, for about 5 minutes until golden brown all over. Drain the fried croquettes on a plate lined with kitchen paper and serve them while they are still hot, garnished with lemon slices.

Tip
Accompany with a Sicilian Birra Messina or another artisan beer.

Small 'fritter' pizzas
Pizzelle

In days gone by, fishermen's wives would take any surplus anchovy catch, or any damaged fish that could not be sold, and mix it into their pizza dough. Over time, these pizzas have evolved into small fritters with raisins, and they really are a treat!

Preparation time: 15 minutes
Resting time: 2 hours 20 minutes
Cooking time: 25 minutes
Serves 4 (makes about 12 fritters)

- 1 small potato, about 125g (4½oz), unpeeled and scrubbed
- 250g (9oz) type '00' flour, plus extra for dusting
- 1 teaspoon salt
- 10g (¼oz) fresh yeast
- 3–4 teaspoons tepid water
- 30g (1oz) raisins
- 50g (1¾oz) anchovy fillets in olive oil, drained and cut into small pieces
- a few rosemary leaves
- oil, for deep-frying

Boil the potato in a saucepan of salted water for about 20 minutes, or until tender. Drain, and when cool enough to handle, peel off the skin and mash the potato.

Sift the flour and salt into a large bowl and add the mashed potato. Crumble the yeast into the tepid water in a small cup and stir to dissolve. Make a well in the centre of the potato and flour mixture and pour in the dissolved yeast. Knead everything together with your hands to make a smooth dough. Shape it into a ball, cover with clingfilm and leave to rest until the dough has doubled in volume, about 2 hours.

Turn out the dough onto a lightly dusted work surface and stretch it out with your hands to flatten. Sprinkle the dough with the raisins and chopped anchovies and press these firmly into the dough. Fold the dough in three, envelope-fashion, bringing up the bottom third, then folding over the top third. Using your hands, shape it into balls the size of large walnuts. Place on a baking sheet, cover with a cloth and leave to rise for about 20 minutes until well risen.

Add the rosemary leaves to a deep-sided saucepan with enough oil for deep-frying. Heat to 180–190°C (350–375°F), or until a cube of bread browns in 30 seconds. Deep-fry the balls, in batches, until golden brown, then drain on a plate lined with kitchen paper. Serve immediately.

Tips

If you prefer, you can use a good-quality ready-made pizza dough.

Enjoy the fritters hot with a sparkling white wine.

Arancini

Arancini are now widely known outside Italy, but their origins probably less so. In Palermo, Sicily's capital, on 13 December, Santa Lucia's feast day is celebrated. No bread or pasta is eaten, only *cuccìa* (a dish of boiled wheatberries and sugar) and rice. So we don't need to give up the delights of arancini! Balilla is a small round-grain rice that is farmed organically in Italy. If you cannot find it, use Arborio or Carnaroli risotto rice.

Preparation time: 40 minutes
Cooking time: 1 hour 25 minutes
Serves 6

- 100–150ml (3½–5fl oz) olive oil
- 2 garlic cloves, peeled and left whole
- 250g (9oz) minced beef
- 500g (1lb 2oz) passata
- 140g (5oz) frozen peas
- 6 basil leaves
- 3 teaspoons sugar
- 500g (1lb 2oz) small, round-grain Italian rice, preferably Balilla
- 2 pinches of saffron threads
- 3 eggs, separated
- 100g (3½oz) grated Parmesan cheese
- 100g (3½oz) dry breadcrumbs
- oil, for deep-frying
- salt and freshly ground black pepper

Heat the olive oil in a small flameproof casserole over a medium heat and fry the garlic cloves until golden. Add the minced beef, crushing it with a fork to break up any lumps. Add the passata, peas, basil leaves, sugar and 300ml (10fl oz) of water. Season with salt and pepper and leave to simmer for about 30 minutes until thickened. Remove the garlic cloves, then leave to cool.

While the mixture cools, cook the rice following the packet instructions, adding the saffron threads and a pinch of salt to the measured water (allow three times the volume of water to rice). After 20–25 minutes, check the rice – it should have absorbed the water completely.

Tip the cooked rice into a large bowl, add the egg yolks and grated Parmesan and mix well.

Lightly beat the egg whites in a separate bowl until frothy. Dip the palm of your hand in the whites and cover with a generous portion of the rice mixture. Place a small spoonful of the meat mixture in the centre and shape the rice around the meat to enclose it, adding a little more rice if necessary. Shape into a ball the size of a small orange. Repeat using the remaining meat mixture and rice to make 6 balls. Coat each one in the breadcrumbs.

Heat enough oil for deep-frying in a deep-sided saucepan to 180–190°C (350–375°F), or until a cube of bread browns in 30 seconds. Deep-fry the balls until golden brown all over. Drain on a plate lined with kitchen paper and serve warm.

Tips

If you have any leftover saffron risotto, you can use it to make this dish.

Serve with a full-bodied red wine, such as Sicilian Nero d'Avola.

Chickpea pancake

Farinata di ceci

This pancake, originally brought to Sicily by the Genoese, has also become a speciality of Liguria province in northwest Italy. The Sicilians turned it into a *panelle*, a kind of doughnut made from chickpea flour. When I serve it, I like to add a few drops of lemon juice.

Preparation time: 10 minutes
Resting time: 5 hours
Cooking time: 15–20 minutes
Serves 4–6

- 300g (10½oz) chickpea flour
- 1 teaspoon salt
- 2 tablespoons olive oil, plus extra for greasing
- 1 litre (1¾ pints/4¼ cups) water
- a squeeze of lemon juice, to serve (optional)

Put the chickpea flour, salt and olive oil in a mixing bowl. Add the water a little at a time, whisking constantly. Cover the bowl with clingfilm and leave the batter to rest at room temperature for about 5 hours.

When you're ready to cook, preheat the oven to 180°C (350°F), Gas Mark 4. Transfer the batter to a well-oiled baking tray or divide between 2 well-oiled springform tins, 26–28cm (10½–11in) diameter. Bake for 15–20 minutes and serve hot with a squeeze of lemon juice, if you wish. Enjoy with aperitifs.

Tips

If you wish, flavour the batter with cumin (seeds or ground). You can also add vegetables, such as sliced courgettes, peas and fresh broad beans that have been sautéed in a pan with a little olive oil, chopped garlic, salt, freshly ground pepper and chopped fresh herbs.

Accompany with an Etna Rosato Donnafugata wine or another fragrant rosé.

Sicilian chickpea fritters

Panelle siciliane

Preparation time: 10 minutes
Cooking time: 40 minutes
Makes 40

- 500g (1lb 2oz) chickpea flour
- 20g (¾oz) salt
- about 1.4 litres (2½ pints/scant 6 cups) water
- 15 flat-leaf parsley sprigs, finely chopped
- oil, for deep-frying

Tip the chickpea flour and salt into a large saucepan and stir to mix. Add the water, a little at a time, whisking constantly to avoid lumps forming. The consistency of the batter must be quite liquid and runny. Gently heat the mixture, still stirring constantly with a whisk. Remove the saucepan from the heat and mix in the parsley, then continue cooking, stirring briskly all the time. It will take about 30 minutes for the batter to reach a homogeneous consistency.

Spread the batter, 5mm (¼in) thick, over a lightly oiled baking tray and leave to cool, then cut into roughly 5cm (2in) squares.

Heat enough oil for deep-frying in a deep-sided saucepan to 180–190°C (350–375°F), or until a cube of bread browns in 30 seconds. Deep-fry the fritters, in batches, until golden brown – they should be crisp on the outside but soft inside. Drain on a plate lined with kitchen paper and serve hot with aperitifs.

Sicilian pizza 'rianella'
Pizza siciliana 'rianella'

The traditional Sicilian pizza 'arianata' from Trapani reminds me of summer get-togethers at my cousins' house by the sea. The name 'arianata' comes from *rieno*, meaning oregano in Sicilian dialect (in Italian this pizza is *origanata*). I've given it a modern twist by using mozzarella as well as the traditional pecorino cheese, hence the new name 'rianella'. If time is tight, use readymade pizza dough.

Preparation time: 15 minutes
Rising time: 3½ hours
Cooking time: 15 minutes
Serves 6

For homemade dough:
- 25g (1oz) fresh yeast
- 250ml (9fl oz) tepid water
- 1 teaspoon sugar
- 500g (1lb 2oz) type '00' flour, plus extra for kneading
- 2 teaspoons salt
- 5 tablespoons olive oil, plus extra for greasing

For the topping:
- 2 × 400g (14oz) cans of San Marzano peeled plum tomatoes
- 6 tablespoons olive oil, plus extra for drizzling
- pinch of salt
- 4 tablespoons chopped Sicilian oregano
- 80g (2¾oz) canned anchovy fillets in olive oil, drained and chopped into small pieces
- 3 large garlic cloves, finely sliced
- 12 flat-leaf parsley sprigs, finely chopped
- 200g (7oz) grated Sicilian pecorino cheese
- 150g (5½oz) cows' milk mozzarella, sliced

To prepare the dough, crumble the yeast into a glass containing about 50ml (2fl oz) of the tepid water, stirring all the time with a wooden spoon. Add the sugar and 2–3 tablespoons of the flour. Stir briskly together to make a shiny, smooth dough. Transfer it to a bowl, cover with a tea towel and leave to rise in a warm place for about 30 minutes.

Sift the remaining flour into a separate bowl, make a well in the centre and put the risen dough in it. Add the salt, sprinkling it just over the flour around the outside of the bowl (the salt must not come into immediate contact with the yeast), then the olive oil, and the remaining 200ml (7fl oz) of tepid water. Begin by working the ingredients together with your hands, very gradually drawing in the flour towards the middle. Transfer the dough to a lightly floured work surface and knead for at least 5 minutes. If the dough is too firm, add an extra 1–2 tablespoons of tepid water; if it is too soft, add a little extra flour. Shape the dough into a ball, dust lightly with flour and place in a clean bowl. Cut a cross in the top. Cover the dough with a damp tea towel and leave it to rise for about 2 hours or until doubled in volume.

Once the dough has risen, begin to spread it out with your hands, working from the middle outwards, until it has a thickness of at least 1cm (½in). Lift the dough onto a well-oiled baking sheet and press it outwards with your fingers until it reaches the edges of the sheet. Cover again with the tea towel and leave to rise for at least another hour.

When you are ready to cook, preheat the oven to 220°C (425°F), Gas Mark 7.

To prepare the topping, crush the plum tomatoes in a bowl and stir through the olive oil, salt and 2 tablespoons of the oregano. Arrange the chopped anchovies over the dough, followed by the sliced garlic, ensuring they stick to the dough. Spoon over the tomato mixture and sprinkle with the chopped parsley, grated pecorino, the remaining oregano and a generous drizzle of oil.

Bake the pizza for about 10 minutes. Remove from the oven, arrange the mozzarella slices on top and bake for a further 3 minutes. Slice and serve.

Sicilian focaccia

Fuazze alla siciliana

It's not so long ago that this bread was barely known outside Italy, but today it's as popular as pizza! The Sicilian version is filled with the finest produce grown on the island.

Preparation time: 20 minutes
Cooking time: 40 minutes
Serves 4–6

- 7 tablespoons olive oil, plus extra for greasing
- 1kg (2lb 4oz) red onions, preferably Tropea (a very sweet Italian red variety), chopped
- 1 tablespoon fennel seeds
- 200g (7oz) cherry tomatoes, halved
- 1 tablespoon dried oregano
- 1 quantity of good-quality readymade pizza dough (or use the recipe on page 30)
- 300g (10½oz) canned tuna (see Tip), drained
- salt and freshly ground black pepper

Heat 5–6 tablespoons of the olive oil in a sauté pan and gently fry the onions with half of the fennel seeds and a pinch of salt, adding 50ml (2fl oz) water to the pan. Continue to cook until the onions have caramelized. Add the halved cherry tomatoes, another pinch of salt, freshly ground pepper and half of the oregano. Simmer for about 5 minutes.

Preheat the oven to 200°C (400°F), Gas Mark 6.

Roll out half of the pizza dough thinly on an oiled baking sheet. Spread the onion and tuna, broken into large flakes, over it. Roll out the remaining dough thinly on a lightly floured work surface and lift it over the filling (as if you were making a pie). Seal the dough edges firmly by folding them over towards the centre.

Brush the remaining olive oil over the dough, sprinkle with salt, the rest of the oregano and fennel seeds. Bake for about 20 minutes and enjoy warm from the oven.

Tips

If possible, use tuna fillets that are canned in natural spring water or olive oil, as these have the best flavour.

Serve the focaccia with a Birra Messina or another artisan beer.

Sweet-and-sour pumpkin
Zucca in agrodolce

In Sicily, this is a traditional autumn dish with a delicious flavour and intoxicating aroma. It can be served cold as a starter or as an accompaniment to a main dish, such as grilled fish.

Preparation time: 15 minutes
Cooking time: 20 minutes
Serves 4–6

- 1kg (2lb 4oz) pumpkin, peeled and seeds and fibres removed
- 100ml (3½fl oz) grapeseed oil or other vegetable oil
- 50ml (2fl oz) olive oil
- 2 garlic cloves, chopped
- 3 tablespoons sugar
- 3 tablespoons wine vinegar
- small bunch of fresh mint, leaves picked
- 20g (¾oz) flaked almonds, toasted
- salt and freshly ground black pepper

Cut the pumpkin flesh into 5cm (2in) cubes. Heat the grapeseed and olive oils in a large frying pan and fry the pumpkin on all sides until tender and slightly golden. Remove the cubes using a slotted spoon, leaving the oil in the pan.

Add the garlic, sugar, vinegar and mint leaves (reserving some to garnish) to the pan, season with salt and pepper and bring to the boil. Return the pumpkin cubes to the pan and simmer for 3 minutes. Remove from the heat, transfer to a serving dish and leave to cool.

Sprinkle over the flaked almonds and reserved mint leaves and serve well chilled.

Tip

Accompany with a Rosato di Nerello Mascalese or another Sicilian rosé wine.

Aubergine caponata
Caponata palermitaine

Sicily's famous Violette aubergines take centre stage here. Caponata can be eaten warm, but I prefer it cold, as it releases more aromas! I use salted capers as they are more flavoursome.

Preparation time:
25 minutes
Soaking time: 40 minutes
Cooking time: 25 minutes
Serves 6

- 6 round Sicilian Violette aubergines or long aubergines, washed
- oil, for shallow- or deep-frying
- 2 tablespoons salted capers (find them in your local Italian deli)
- 30g (1oz) raisins
- 150g (5½oz) celery sticks, chopped small
- 100g (3½oz) black olives, pitted and rinsed
- 100ml (3½fl oz) olive oil
- 1 large onion, finely chopped
- 2 garlic cloves
- 300g (10½oz) passata or canned chopped tomatoes
- 1 tablespoon sugar
- 50ml (2fl oz) wine vinegar
- 30g (1oz) pine nuts
- 1 teaspoon unsweetened cocoa powder
- salt and freshly ground black pepper
- basil leaves, to garnish

Cut the aubergines into large cubes. Put in a bowl of salted water and leave to soak for about 30 minutes. Drain the cubes and pat dry thoroughly with kitchen paper. Pour enough oil (you can shallow- or deep-fry) into a deep-sided saucepan and heat to 180–190°C (350–375°F), or until a cube of bread browns in 30 seconds. Add the aubergine, in batches, and cook until tender and golden brown. Drain on kitchen paper and set aside.

Soak the salted capers and the raisins in a bowl of cold water for about 10 minutes.

Add the celery and olives to a saucepan of hot water and simmer for about 3 minutes. Drain immediately.

Heat the olive oil in a flameproof casserole over a medium heat and fry the onion and whole garlic cloves until golden. Add the passata or chopped tomatoes, sugar and vinegar and stir with a wooden spoon. Simmer over a gentle heat for about 10 minutes. Add the pine nuts, drained capers and raisins, olives and celery and dust with the cocoa powder. If it looks at all dry, add 75ml (2½fl oz) of water while cooking.

Lastly, add the fried aubergines and simmer for a further 5 minutes. Remove the garlic cloves.

Season with salt and pepper and serve with some fresh basil leaves.

Tips

Serve warm or cold as a side dish or a starter.

Accompany with an Etna Rosso DOC, or another Sicilian red wine.

Caponata pie
Pasticcio di caponata

Caponata is terrific as a filling in this simple pie using ready-rolled shortcrust pastry. You can also make this pie with pizza dough, but it must be rolled out thinly on a well-floured work surface.

Preparation time: 15 minutes
Cooking time: 35 minutes
Serves 4

- 2 × 250g (8oz) sheets of ready-rolled shortcrust pastry
- 400g (14oz) Caponata (see page 39)
- 150g (5½oz) fresh Sicilian pecorino, cut into slices
- 1 egg yolk, beaten

Preheat the oven to 180°C (350°F), Gas Mark 4.

Use one sheet of pastry to line a deep-sided 26–28cm (10½–11in) tart tin, allowing the edges of the pastry to overhang. Drain the caponata thoroughly (if there is too much liquid), then spoon into the pastry case and scatter over the fresh pecorino slices. Cover the filling with the second pastry sheet. Trim the pastry edges, if necessary, and fold the overhang in towards the centre so the rim of the pie is tightly sealed. Cut a small hole in the pastry lid to allow steam to escape during baking.

Brush the top of the pie with the beaten egg yolk and bake for around 35 minutes.

Tips

You can replace the pecorino with mozzarella slices.

Accompany with an Etna Rosso DOC or another Sicilian red wine.

Chard and fennel pie
Torta di bietole e finocchietto

This starter is perfect for vegetarians as long as you leave out the anchovies. Wild fennel sprigs are unusual outside of Italy. If you struggle to source them, use the leafy tops that are attached to fresh fennel bulbs.

Preparation time: 30 minutes
Chilling time: 30 minutes
Cooking time: 50 minutes
Serves 4–6

For the pastry:
- 250g (9oz) plain flour
- 125g (4½oz) butter, cut into small dice, plus extra for greasing
- pinch of salt
- 50ml (2fl oz) cold water

For the filling:
- 1.5kg (3lb 5oz) chard
- 4-5 tablespoons olive oil
- 2 garlic cloves, sliced
- 4 anchovy fillets in olive oil, chopped (optional)
- a few sprigs of fresh wild fennel or from a jar
- 500g (1lb 2oz) sheep's milk ricotta cheese
- 30g (1oz) raisins
- 30g (1oz) pine nuts
- 3 eggs, beaten
- salt and freshly ground black pepper

To prepare the pastry, using a food mixer, beat the flour with the butter and salt. When the mixture has a crumbly texture, add the measured water and continue to mix until you have a smooth dough (you may need a little extra water). Shape the dough into a ball, wrap in clingfilm and chill for 30 minutes in the refrigerator.

To prepare the filling, cook the chard in a saucepan of salted boiling water for about 10 minutes. Drain and cut into small pieces.

Heat the olive oil in a frying pan and gently fry the sliced garlic until golden. Add the chopped anchovies (if using) and chard and fry for a few minutes. Add the wild fennel, season with salt and pepper and set aside to cool until lukewarm.

Add the ricotta to the cooled chard, mixing it in by crushing with a fork, then the raisins, pine nuts, eggs (reserving a little egg to glaze the pastry lattice) and 1 tablespoon of water.

Preheat the oven to 180°C (350°F), Gas Mark 4.

Grease a 20-22cm (8-9in) tart tin with butter. Roll out the pastry and use it to line the tin, trimming the edges neatly and reserving the pastry trimmings. Spoon the chard filling into the pastry case. Gather together and re-roll the trimmings and cut into strips using a fluted pizza wheel. Arrange these over the pie in a lattice pattern, dampening the ends to fix them in place. Dilute the remaining beaten egg with 1 tablespoon of water and brush it over the pastry strips.

Bake for around 40 minutes. Serve in generous slices.

Tips
Accompany with an Etna Rosato Donnafugata or another Sicilian rosé wine.

Nonna's stuffed aubergines
Melanzane della nonna

Aubergines are in season between July and September and, when summer arrives, I can't wait to make this recipe for my guests. I prepare it the day before and the result is irresistible!

Preparation time: 30 minutes
Resting time: overnight
Cooking time: 1 hour 5 minutes
Serves 4

- 5 long Violette aubergines or long aubergines
- 100ml (3½fl oz) olive oil, plus extra for greasing and drizzling
- 1 red onion, finely chopped
- 2 garlic cloves, finely chopped
- 80g (2¾oz) jarred anchovy fillets in olive oil
- 3 tablespoons capers
- 15 flat-leaf parsley sprigs, chopped
- 3 tablespoons passata
- 80g (2¾oz) grated Parmesan cheese
- 50g (1¾oz) dry breadcrumbs
- 3 eggs
- 50ml (2fl oz) white balsamic vinegar
- 1 quantity of Sicilian Tomato Sauce (see page 52)
- salt

The day before, cut the aubergines in half lengthways. Using a spoon, scrape out the flesh and reserve. Put the aubergine shells in a large saucepan, cover with cold salted water, bring to the boil and cook for 2–3 minutes. Drain immediately and let the shells cool.

Cut the reserved flesh into small pieces. Heat the olive oil in a large sauté pan and fry the onion and garlic until lightly browned. Add the aubergine flesh and mix well. Next, add the anchovies, capers, chopped parsley and passata. Cook over a low heat for 10 minutes, then remove from the heat. Once cool, add the grated Parmesan, breadcrumbs and 1 of the eggs and stir until evenly combined. Set aside.

Hard-boil the remaining 2 eggs in a pan of boiling water for about 10 minutes. Plunge into cold water before shelling, then cut each egg into 4 or 5 pieces.

Preheat the oven to 180°C (350°F), Gas Mark 4.

Oil an ovenproof dish, large enough to accommodate all the aubergine shells (or use two dishes). Arrange the aubergine shells in a single layer. Divide the chopped egg between them, then fill each shell with the cooked aubergine mixture. Drizzle each one with a little olive oil and bake for about 30 minutes.

As soon as the aubergines come out of the oven, sprinkle with a few drops of white balsamic vinegar and coat with the tomato sauce. Allow to rest overnight and serve cold the following day.

Tip
Serve with a Nerello Mascalese Rosso or another Sicilian red wine.

Seafood salad

Insalata di mare

This salad appears regularly on the menus of seaside restaurants. Personally, I have a slight preference for the version made just with octopus (see below). It is essential to buy fresh octopus – and rock octopus is best!

Preparation time: 30 minutes
Chilling time: 2 hours
Cooking time: 1 hour
Serves 6

- 1 fresh octopus, weighing about 1.5kg (3lb 5oz)
- 1kg (2lb 4oz) clams
- 2 garlic cloves, chopped
- 20 flat-leaf parsley sprigs, half finely chopped
- 150–180ml (5–6¼fl oz) olive oil
- 50ml (2fl oz) dry white wine
- 700g (1lb 9oz) mussels
- 300g (10½oz) raw prawns, heads removed
- 500g (1lb 2oz) fresh cuttlefish, cleaned and prepared
- juice of 1 lemon
- 4 tablespoons black Taggiasche olives, pitted
- 3 celery sticks, cut into small pieces
- 6 cherry tomatoes, halved
- salt and freshly ground black pepper

Bring a large saucepan or stockpot of water to the boil, then plunge the octopus into it three times without completely submerging it. The fourth time, immerse the octopus completely and cook for 45 minutes, then turn off the heat, add salt to the water and leave the octopus to cool in it.

Wash the clams and soak them in a bowl of salted water, changing the water frequently (4 or 5 times). Drain, then add the clams to a large, lidded stockpot, along with the garlic, the whole parsley sprigs, 5–6 tablespoons of the olive oil and the wine. Bring to a gentle boil and cook, covered, for 3–4 minutes, stirring occasionally with a wooden spoon. Remove the clams from the pot and set aside, leaving the cooking juices in the pot.

Wash and clean the mussels and boil them for 3–4 minutes in the same stockpot used for the clams, covered. Remove the mussels and set aside, reserving the juices. Cook the prawns in a separate pan of boiling water for 1–2 minutes. Drain and peel off their shells. Rinse the cuttlefish, then place in a pan of cold water. Bring to the boil and cook for 7 minutes, then drain and set aside to cool.

Meanwhile, remove most of the clams and mussels from their shells, keeping a few unshelled for garnish. Once cool, cut the cuttlefish and the octopus into small pieces. Mix together.

Pour the remaining olive oil into a large bowl, then add the lemon juice, chopped parsley, olives, celery, octopus, cuttlefish, the shelled prawns, clams and mussels and 75ml (2½fl oz) of the reserved clam juices. Mix everything together and chill for at least 2 hours.

Spoon the seafood salad onto individual plates or one large serving platter, placing the unshelled mussels and clams on top, along with the tomatoes. Serve well chilled.

Tip

Accompany with a Mandrarossa Grillo Bianco or another Sicilian white wine.

A Mediterranean variation

Cook the octopus, as above. Leave it to cool and then cut into small pieces. Add the olive oil, lemon juice, chopped parsley, olives and celery to a large bowl with 2 tablespoons of harissa and 3 tablespoons of capers. Add the octopus, mix well and refrigerate for at least 1 hour.

Sicilian parmigiana
Parmigiana siciliana

This is different from the recipe from Parma as it adds meat and eggs (a Greek legacy), which makes it even richer. It makes a perfect picnic dish.

Preparation time: 30 minutes
Soaking time: 30 minutes
Cooking time: 1 hour 10 minutes
Serves 6

- 5–6 medium aubergines
- 90ml (6 tablespoons) olive oil, for frying or baking
- 250g (9oz) minced veal or beef
- 1 garlic clove
- 2 whole cloves
- 15g (½oz) butter
- 100g (3½oz) dry breadcrumbs
- 80g (2¾oz) grated Parmesan cheese
- 3 basil leaves, chopped
- 2 hard-boiled eggs, shelled and sliced
- 250g (9oz) fresh Sicilian pecorino or white scamorza cheese, thinly sliced
- 100g (3½oz) thinly sliced mortadella
- 2 eggs
- salt and freshly ground black pepper

For the Sicilian tomato sauce:
- 90ml (6 tablespoons) olive oil
- 2 garlic cloves
- 500g (1lb 2oz) passata
- 2 basil leaves, torn
- 1 teaspoon sugar

Cut the aubergines into 1–2cm (½–¾in) slices and soak in a bowl of salted water for 30 minutes. Drain, then pat dry with kitchen paper. Now either gently fry them in 6 tablespoons of olive oil until softened and golden on both sides or place on a baking tray, brush with a little of the olive oil and bake in the oven at 180°C (350°F), Gas Mark 4 for about 25 minutes (baking them uses less oil). Set aside.

Meanwhile, make the tomato sauce. Heat 2 tablespoons of the olive oil in a flameproof casserole and gently fry the whole garlic cloves. Add the passata, basil leaves and sugar and season with salt and pepper. Simmer for 15 minutes, adding 100ml (3½fl oz) of water, if necessary.

In a separate frying pan, fry the garlic clove and whole cloves in 3 or 4 tablespoons of olive oil. Add the minced meat, breaking any lumps up with a fork. Cook for 2–3 minutes and then remove the whole cloves. Tip the meat into the tomato sauce and simmer for a further 5 minutes before removing the casserole from the heat.

Preheat the oven to 180°C (350°F), Gas Mark 4.

Grease an ovenproof dish with the butter and dust with dry breadcrumbs, reserving some of the crumbs for the topping. Add the ingredients in the following order: a layer of aubergine slices (reserve enough for a final layer), meat sauce, Parmesan (reserve some for the topping), chopped basil, sliced hard-boiled eggs, fresh pecorino or scamorza, then the mortadella, and finish with a final layer of aubergine slices.

Beat the 2 eggs with the reserved grated Parmesan and spoon it over the aubergine slices to coat. Dust with the reserved breadcrumbs.

Bake for about 25 minutes until a golden crust forms on top. Allow to stand for 5 minutes, then serve, or allow to cool completely.

Tips

Sicilian parmigiana is also excellent when served cold.

Accompany it with a Nerello Cappuccio Rosso or another Sicilian red wine.

Pasta

Penne with pistachios and bottarga

Penne con pistachi e bottarga

This recipe contains two key ingredients: pistachios and bottarga. In France, where I live, and in the UK and USA, grey mullet bottarga is the most readily available and I've used it here. Sicilian cooks use tuna bottarga, which is traditional in the Trapani region, but it has a different texture, is saltier and more expensive than the mullet version.

Preparation time: 15 minutes
Marinating time: 10 minutes
Cooking time: 15 minutes
Serves 4

- 1 red onion, finely chopped
- juice of 1 lemon
- 150ml (5fl oz) olive oil
- 1 garlic clove, crushed
- 50g (1¾oz) raw pistachios, shelled and roughly crushed
- 2 beefsteak tomatoes, cut into small dice
- 50g (1¾oz) grey mullet bottarga
- 500g (1lb 2oz) mini penne
- salt and freshly ground black pepper

Season the onion and squeeze over half of the lemon juice.

Heat 90ml (6 tablespoons) of the olive oil in a large frying pan over a medium heat and fry the garlic and onion for 2 minutes until golden. Add the pistachios, fry for 1 minute, then add the diced tomatoes. Stir together over a high heat for 1 minute (but no longer), then remove from the heat.

Thinly slice half of the bottarga and marinate in the remaining olive oil for 5–10 minutes.

Meanwhile, cook the penne in a pan of boiling, salted water until al dente. Drain, tip the pasta into the frying pan and place it over a gentle heat. Mix everything together and grate over the remaining bottarga.

When ready to serve, squeeze over the remaining lemon juice and top the pasta with the marinated bottarga slices. Serve immediately.

Tip

Accompany with a Sicilia Menfi DOC Chardonnay or another Sicilian white wine.

Bucatini with sardines
Bucatini con le sarde

This dish was created during the Arab occupation of Sicily between the 9th and the 11th centuries, when the use of dried fruits and spices (especially saffron) was common. The custom later became part of the cuisine, along with the addition of sardines, which are abundant in the island's waters. Don't forget to plan a trip to the countryside to pick wild fennel (a childhood memory for me)!

Preparation time: 30 minutes
Soaking time: 15 minutes
Cooking time: 45 minutes
Serves 4

- a beautiful bunch of fresh wild fennel (or from a jar)
- 400g (14oz) fresh sardines
- 150ml (5fl oz) olive oil, plus extra as needed
- 1 onion, chopped
- 1 large tablespoon raisins
- 30g (1oz) pine nuts
- 5 anchovy fillets in olive oil
- 150ml (5fl oz) passata
- 2 pinches of saffron
- 400g (14oz) bucatini
- 50g (1¾oz) dried breadcrumbs
- a few flaked almonds
- salt and freshly ground black pepper

If using fresh fennel, wash the leaves, plunge them into a saucepan of boiling water and cook for about 15 minutes. Drain, reserving the cooking liquid, and chop the fennel fronds finely.

Clean and debone the sardines, keeping only the fillets. Rinse, pat dry and season with salt and pepper, then fry the fillets in the olive oil in a large frying pan until golden. Remove the fillets and set aside, reserving the oil in the pan.

In the same pan, gently fry the onion for a few minutes (add a little more oil if needed). Add the raisins, pine nuts, anchovies, finely chopped fennel fronds, passata, saffron, salt and pepper and 2 ladlefuls of the fennel cooking water. Cover and simmer for about 10 minutes. Return the sardines to the pan and cook for a further 10 minutes.

Meanwhile, cook the bucatini until al dente in a saucepan of boiling, salted water, adding the reserved fennel cooking liquid.

In a separate frying pan, fry the breadcrumbs in a drizzle of olive oil.

Drain the pasta and tip it into the frying pan with the sauce. Sprinkle with a few flaked almonds and the breadcrumbs and serve immediately.

Tips

If you cannot find wild fennel, save the leafy tops of fennel bulbs. You can also grate Sicilian pecorino cheese over the dish.

Accompany with a Mandrarossa Grillo Bianco or another Sicilian white wine.

Casarecce with aubergines and ricotta salata
Casarecce alla Norma

There are two key ingredients in this pasta dish: aubergines and ricotta salata – a cheese you will only find in Italian delicatessens. The recipe originates from the city of Catania on Italy's east coast, where it was dedicated to the opera *Norma* by Vincenzo Bellini.

Preparation time: 15 minutes
Soaking time: 30 minutes
Cooking time: 1 hour
Serves 4

- 2 large round aubergines
- 150ml (5fl oz) olive oil
- 2 garlic cloves
- 700ml (1¼ pints) passata
- 4 teaspoons sugar
- 12 basil leaves, plus extra to garnish
- 700ml (1¼ pints) cold water
- oil, for frying the aubergines
- 500g (1lb 2oz) casarecce (a Sicilian pasta)
- 120g (4½oz) ricotta salata cheese (firm ricotta), shaved into curls or coarsely grated
- salt and freshly ground black pepper

Cut the aubergines into large cubes and leave them to soak in a bowl of salted water for about 30 minutes.

Heat the olive oil in a flameproof casserole over a medium heat and fry the whole garlic cloves for a few minutes. When they are golden, add the passata, sugar, basil leaves and the measured cold water. Season with salt and pepper. Simmer over a gentle heat for 1 hour with a lid half-covering the pan.

Drain and pat dry the aubergines with kitchen paper. Heat enough oil either for shallow-frying in a wide frying pan or for deep-frying in a deep-sided saucepan to 180–190°C (350–375°F), or until a cube of bread browns in 30 seconds. Shallow- or deep-fry the aubergines until browned, then remove and set aside.

Cook the casarecce in a saucepan of salted boiling water until al dente, then drain and tip into the tomato sauce, mixing well. Add the fried aubergines and the ricotta salata.

Serve immediately, garnished with extra basil leaves.

Tips

You can use penne instead of casarecce.

Accompany with a Nero d'Avola red wine.

Oven-baked pasta
Pasta al forno

This recipe, originally from Naples, is unusual in that it contains fried aubergines, hard-boiled eggs and an Italian hard cheese called caciocavallo in addition to the typical meat-based sauce. A symbolic dish, it's perfect for bringing all the family together for Sunday lunch.

Preparation time: 40 minutes
Cooking time: 1 hour 15 minutes
Serves 4

- 100ml (3½fl oz) olive oil
- 2 garlic cloves
- 250g (9oz) sausagemeat
- 250g (9oz) minced veal
- 280g (10oz) frozen petits pois
- 700ml (1¼ pints) passata
- 10 basil leaves
- 4 teaspoons sugar
- 2 aubergines, sliced
- 400g (14oz) rigatoni
- 100g (3½oz) grated Parmesan cheese, plus extra to garnish
- 200g (7oz) smoked scamorza cheese, cut into small pieces
- 4 eggs
- 2 hard-boiled eggs
- 30g (1oz) butter, plus extra to top
- 50g (1¾oz) dried breadcrumbs, plus extra to top
- 4 mortadella slices, julienned
- 200g (7oz) fresh caciocavallo cheese (or use cows' milk mozzarella), thinly sliced
- rocket, extra basil leaves and confit tomatoes, to garnish
- salt and black pepper

Heat half of the olive oil in a flameproof casserole and fry the whole garlic cloves over a medium heat until golden. Add the sausagemeat and minced veal, crushing the meats with a fork to break up any lumps. Next, add the peas, passata, basil, sugar and 500ml (18fl oz) cold water and season with salt and pepper. Simmer for 45 minutes. Heat the remaining olive oil in a frying pan and fry the sliced aubergines until golden brown. Drain on kitchen paper.

Cook the rigatoni in a saucepan of salted boiling water until al dente, then drain and tip into a large bowl. Add a few ladlefuls of the meat ragù, 80g (2¾oz) of the grated Parmesan and the scamorza. Beat 3 of the eggs and add to the bowl. Season with salt and pepper and stir until the ingredients are well combined.

Preheat the oven to 180°C (350°F), Gas Mark 4. Shell and slice the hard-boiled eggs.

Grease a deep ovenproof hinged mould or springform cake tin with the butter and dust it with the breadcrumbs. Add a layer of pasta and mortadella strips. Top with half of the fried aubergine, followed by half of the hard-boiled eggs, then half of the caciocavallo and a little more meat ragù. Repeat these layers a second time. Top the final ragù layer with small flakes of butter, the rest of the Parmesan and a dusting of breadcrumbs. Beat the remaining egg and spread it over everything – it will form a crust during baking.

Bake your layered pasta for about 30 minutes. To stop it drying out, cover the top with foil halfway through the cooking time, then remove the foil 5 minutes before the end of the cooking time so the top browns and crisps. Leave to stand for a further 5 minutes, then unmould and serve garnished with Parmesan, small rocket leaves, extra basil leaves and confit tomatoes.

Tips

Using a hinged mould or springform cake tin will make turning out the baked pasta easier. Don't worry about what shape it is, the taste is much more important!

Accompany with a Nerello Cappuccio Rosso or another Sicilian red wine.

Busiate with Trapani pesto
Busiate al pesto trapanese

Busiate is an artisan spiral pasta made by hand in Sicily using an ancient wheat variety. My family like to serve the pasta with sardines grilled on a barbecue, a cherished summer memory.

Preparation time:
15 minutes
Cooking time: 10–12 minutes
Serves 4

- 60g (2¼oz) blanched almonds
- 3–4 garlic cloves
- large bunch of fresh basil
- 200ml (7fl oz) olive oil, plus extra if needed
- 500g (1lb 2oz) canned San Marzano peeled tomatoes (or fresh tomatoes, skinned)
- 500g (1lb 2oz) busiate
- 1 teaspoon salt
- 1 teaspoon freshly ground black pepper

Chop the almonds and garlic, then transfer to a food processor. Add the basil, olive oil and half the salt and freshly ground black pepper, and process until smooth. Scrape the pesto into a bowl.

Finely chop the tomatoes, add them to the pesto and mix well. Adjust the seasoning by adding as much of the remaining salt and freshly ground black pepper as you see fit and, if necessary, more olive oil.

Cook the busiate in a large saucepan of salted boiling water until al dente. Drain, then combine the hot pasta with the pesto and serve immediately.

Tip

Accompany with a well-chilled Nero d'Avola rosé.

Fusilli with Aeolian Island pesto
Fusilli al pesto aeoliano

- 1 tablespoon salted capers
- bunch of fresh basil
- 20g (¾oz) fresh mint
- ½ garlic clove
- 300g (10½oz) cherry tomatoes
- 1 small fresh chilli
- 30g (1oz) raw pistachios, shelled
- 150ml (5fl oz) olive oil
- 500g (1lb 2oz) fusilli bucati
- salt

Soak the capers in a bowl of cold water for 15 minutes, then drain and pat dry with kitchen paper. Put the capers, basil, mint, garlic, tomatoes, chilli, pistachios and olive oil in a liquidizer or food processor and blend until you have a shiny, smooth pesto. If necessary, add 50ml (2fl oz) of iced water. Scrape the pesto into a bowl.

Cook the fusilli bucati in a large saucepan of salted boiling water until al dente. Drain, reserving a ladleful of the cooking water.

Mix the hot pasta with the Aeolian pesto, adding a small ladleful of the cooking water, if necessary. Serve immediately.

A word on pasta

From one side of Sicily to the other, pasta is the staple diet.

The great classic Sicilian pasta dish Pasta al Forno (see page 64), often called *pasta 'ncasciata* (baked pasta), is a fixture on Sunday lunch tables, especially at Eastertime. Rich in ingredients and bold in flavour, it holds pride of place at Sicilian family gatherings. Between making ravioli with ragù and this recipe, Italian mammas are kept busy for most of the morning, but the effort is well worth it!

Spaghetti with ricotta and pistachios

Spaghetti con ricotta e pistacchi

Simple and easy to make, adding some of the pasta cooking water to the ricotta makes this dish creamier. My family used to use ditaloni pasta – a short pasta shaped like small tubes – which is eaten with a spoon, but here I've used spaghetti. We would also mix a tablespoon of sugar into the ricotta, without adding extra grated cheese... a real indulgence!

Preparation time: 15 minutes
Cooking time: 10–12 minutes
Serves 4

- 500g (1lb 2oz) spaghetti
- 80g (2¾oz) raw pistachios (see Tip), shelled
- 500g (1lb 2oz) ricotta cheese
- 2–3 tablespoons olive oil, plus extra if needed
- 50g (1¾oz) grated Parmesan cheese
- salt and freshly ground black pepper

Cook the spaghetti in a saucepan of salted boiling water until al dente.

Meanwhile, roughly chop the pistachios and set aside. Mash the ricotta in a large bowl using a fork, add a teaspoon of salt, the olive oil, grated Parmesan, freshly ground pepper and several tablespoons of the pasta cooking water.

Once the pasta is al dente, drain and tip into the bowl containing the ricotta mixture. Stir to combine, adding a further 1–2 tablespoons olive oil, if needed. Sprinkle with the chopped pistachios, check the seasoning, and serve immediately.

Tips

If you can find them, use Bronte pistachios. They grow in the volcanic soils of Mount Etna and have an incomparable flavour and aroma.

Accompany the pasta with a Nerello Mascalese Rosso or another Sicilian red wine.

Sicilian cannelloni

Cannelloni alla siciliana

Unlike classic cannelloni, the Sicilian version includes dried fruits and Marsala wine. There are reasonably priced dry Marsalas, which are ideal for cooking.

Preparation time: 30 minutes
Cooking time: 35 minutes
Serves 4

- drizzle of olive oil
- 1 small onion, very finely chopped
- 50ml (2fl oz) dry Marsala wine
- 200ml (7fl oz) double cream (or full-fat crème fraîche)
- 200g (7oz) cooked ham, diced
- 500g (1lb 2oz) sheep's milk ricotta cheese, mashed
- 50g (1¾oz) pine nuts, lightly toasted
- 50g (1¾oz) raisins, soaked for 5 minutes in 120ml (4fl oz) water and drained
- 20 cannelloni tubes (see Tip)
- 15g (½oz) butter
- 1 quantity Sicilian Tomato Sauce (see page 52)
- 100g (3½oz) grated pecorino or Parmesan cheese
- cumin seeds, to sprinkle (optional)
- salt and freshly ground black pepper

To prepare the filling, heat a little olive oil in a flameproof casserole over a medium heat and cook the onion until golden. Add the Marsala and cream, season with salt and pepper, and cook for 2–3 minutes to reduce a little. Add the diced ham, ricotta, pine nuts and raisins, stir to mix everything, then set aside to cool and thicken.

Stuff the cannelloni tubes with the filling.

Preheat the oven to 180°C (350°F), Gas Mark 4.

Use the butter to grease an ovenproof dish that will accommodate all of the cannelloni in a single layer and spread a layer of tomato sauce over the base. Place the filled tubes side by side on top of the sauce. Spoon the remaining sauce over the cannelloni to cover them and pour 50ml (2fl oz) of water around the sides. Top with a good layer of grated pecorino or Parmesan and sprinkle over a few cumin seeds (if using).

Cover the dish with foil and bake for 30 minutes. Leave to cool a little before serving.

Tips

I sometimes prefer to use 10 sheets of fresh lasagne that I cut in half, so they are the right size to roll around the filling (as the pasta is fresh, the cooking time will be reduced to 20 minutes).

Accompany with a Rapitalà or another Sicilian red wine.

Sea urchin roe and artichoke linguine
Linguine ricci e carciofi

The true Sicilian recipe for this dish is based on garlic, parsley, sea urchins and olive oil, and it celebrates the tangy aroma of the sea. This version, made with artichokes, recalls a dinner I had with friends in Sicily and it was from them that I 'stole' this delicious recipe.

Preparation time: 15 minutes
Cooking time: 15 minutes
Serves 4

- 4 Sicilian Violette artichokes
- juice of 1 lemon
- 5–6 tablespoons olive oil
- 2 garlic cloves, sliced
- 15 flat-leaf parsley sprigs, chopped
- 400g (14oz) linguine
- 250g (9oz) sea urchin roe (available in cans from Italian delicatessens)
- salt and freshly ground black pepper

Trim the artichokes, keeping only the hearts. To do this, remove all the tough outer leaves, cut off the stem with a serrated knife, trim the tops and then remove the hairy choke with a spoon. Put the hearts in a bowl and pour over the lemon juice to prevent them discolouring. Cut the hearts into thin slices (or into quarters, but not too thick).

Heat the olive oil in a large frying pan and gently fry the garlic until it is golden. Add the artichokes and three-quarters of the chopped parsley, then mix well over a low heat. Pour in 150ml (5fl oz) of water and leave to cook for around 10 minutes over a gentle heat, stirring frequently.

Meanwhile, cook the linguine in a large saucepan of salted boiling water until al dente. Drain the pasta and reserve a small ladleful of the cooking water.

Tip the pasta into the frying pan and stir over a very gentle heat for a few minutes. Toss everything together and add the sea urchin roe and the reserved cooking liquid, if needed. Season with salt and pepper and simmer for at least 1 minute over a very gentle heat.

Sprinkle over the remaining chopped parsley and serve.

Tip

If you struggle to find Sicilian Violette artichokes, use larger globe artichokes. These should be cut into thinner slices and will take a little longer to cook.

Accompany with a Catarratto Bianco or another Sicilian white wine.

Ricotta-filled ravioli
Raviole alla ricotta

Traditionally, this dish is served with Stufato di Maiale (see page 120), as the contrast between the sweetness of the ricotta and the tomato sauce the pork is stewed in is perfect. This is another unique and convivial dish, but make it easy on yourself by planning ahead!

Preparation time: 40 minutes
Resting time: 30 minutes
Cooking time: 10 minutes, plus 5 minutes for the ravioli
Serves 4

For the filling:
- 500g (1lb 2oz) sheep's milk ricotta
- 1 whole egg, beaten
- 100g (3½oz) grated Parmesan cheese
- ½ tablespoon olive oil
- 300g (10½oz) fresh spinach
- ½ garlic clove, chopped
- salt and freshly ground black pepper

For the ravioli dough:
- 400g (14oz) type '00' flour, plus extra for dusting
- 1 teaspoon salt
- 4 large eggs, beaten

To prepare the filling, mash the ricotta with a fork, add the beaten egg and grated Parmesan and season with salt and pepper.

Heat the olive oil in a pan, add the spinach and garlic and cook for about 10 minutes. Drain well, then add to the ricotta. Mix well and leave to cool.

To prepare the dough, mix together the flour, salt and eggs in a bowl to form a dough. Knead well until smooth, then shape into a ball, wrap in clingfilm and leave to rest for 30 minutes.

Roll out the dough thinly (by hand or using a pasta machine) and cut into sheets, 50cm (20in) long and 10cm (6in) wide. Place small spoonfuls of the filling at regular intervals over one half of each sheet of dough. Fold over the other half of the dough and, using your fingertips, press around each spoonful of filling to expel the air and seal the two layers of dough.

Cut out individual ravioli using a pastry cutter or pasta wheel. Usually, they are either square or half-moon shaped. Press firmly around the edges of each ravioli to seal them tightly. Line a baking sheet with baking paper and dust with flour, then lay the ravioli on it.

Cook the ravioli in a large saucepan of salted boiling water for about 5 minutes, depending on how thick they are. Drain and serve at once (see Tips).

Tips

You can serve the ravioli drizzled with olive oil and sprinkled with grated cheese and small oregano leaves, or with a tomato and basil sauce.

Accompany with a Rapitalà Hugonis Rosso or another Sicilian red wine.

Risottos and couscous

RISOTTI E CÙSCUSU

Fisherman's risotto
Risotto alla pescatore

Risotto is not really a Sicilian speciality, but over the years Sicilians have adopted it and cooked it in their own way with seafood taking centre stage, naturally. My advice is to use only the freshest produce, as it makes all the difference! Also, ideally, prepare the stock yourself, but you can buy it readymade if you are short of time.

Preparation time: 20 minutes
Cooking time: 1 hour
Serves 4

- 400g (14oz) raw prawns
- 4 raw king prawns, shelled but keep the tails on
- 2 onions
- 500g (1lb 2oz) canned chopped tomatoes
- 15 flat-leaf parsley sprigs, chopped, plus extra to garnish
- 1 small red chilli
- 200ml (7fl oz) dry white wine
- 500g (1lb 2oz) mussels
- 500g (1lb 2oz) clams
- 3 garlic cloves
- 200ml (7fl oz) olive oil, plus extra as needed
- 500g (1lb 2oz) squid, cleaned and prepared
- 1 small shallot, finely chopped
- 350g (12oz) Carnaroli rice
- salt and freshly ground black pepper

Tip
Accompany with an Inzolia Bianco or another Sicilian white wine.

Peel the prawns and put their heads and shells in a large saucepan. Chop 1 onion and add to the pan with the chopped tomatoes, a third of the parsley, the chilli, 1 litre (1¾ pints) of water, half of the wine and a pinch of salt. Cook for 20 minutes, then strain the stock, crushing the heads and shells with a spoon to extract their flavour. Reserve the stock.

Clean the mussels and clams and put them in another large pan. Crush 1 garlic clove and add to the pan with a drizzle of olive oil and half of the remaining parsley. Cover the pan tightly and cook over a high heat for 5–6 minutes, stirring occasionally with a wooden spoon, until all the mussel and clam shells open. Strain the cooking juices and add them to the prawn stock. Remove most of the mussels and clams from their shells, but keep a few in their shells for garnish.

Cut the squid into small pieces, including the heads. Finely chop 1 garlic clove and the remaining onion and fry in 100ml (3½fl oz) olive oil for about 10 minutes. Add the squid and the rest of the parsley, season with salt and pepper and fry over a medium heat for 5 minutes. Set aside.

Heat 100ml (3½fl oz) olive oil in a large sauté pan or large, deep frying pan over a medium heat. Fry the remaining whole garlic clove and the shallot until golden, then remove the garlic and add the rice. Fry until the rice develops a pearly sheen, pour in the rest of the wine and leave until it has evaporated. Reheat the stock, if necessary, and add it to the pan a ladleful at a time, allowing the rice to absorb the stock before adding another ladleful (if you do not have enough stock, you can use hot water for the final additions). Continue to cook for about 18–20 minutes, stirring frequently, until the rice is al dente. Towards the end of the cooking time, add the raw prawns (not the king prawns) and squid.

Heat a little oil in a frying pan and fry the king prawns until they turn pink.

A few minutes before the rice is ready, add the shelled mussels and clams to the rice pan and stir through to reheat.

Remove the pan from the heat, garnish with the unshelled mussels and clams, the king prawns and a few parsley sprigs. Serve immediately.

Grilled octopus and ginger risotto

Risotto al polpo arrostito e allo zenzero

I discovered this more up-to-date version of a recipe that uses black wholegrain (Venere) rice and ginger at a friend's restaurant in Sicily.

Preparation time: 30 minutes
Cooking time: 1 hour 40 minutes
Serves 4

- 1kg (2lb 4oz) octopus
- 350g (12oz) black (Venere) rice
- 225ml (8fl oz) olive oil
- 2 shallots, finely chopped
- 100ml (3½fl oz) dry white wine
- 1 teaspoon grated fresh root ginger
- 1 garlic clove, chopped
- 1 teaspoon finely grated lemon zest and the juice of ½ lemon
- small bunch of flat-leaf parsley, leaves picked
- small bunch of fennel, fronds picked
- salt and freshly ground black pepper

Bring a large stockpot of water to the boil, then plunge the octopus into it three times without completely submerging it. The fourth time, immerse the octopus completely and cook for 45 minutes, then turn off the heat, add salt to the water and leave the octopus to cool in it. Drain, reserving the cooking water and reheating it when needed for making the risotto.

Cook the rice in a saucepan of salted boiling water for 30 minutes until al dente, then drain.

Heat half of the olive oil in a sauté pan over a medium heat and fry the shallots until golden. Cut half of the octopus into small pieces and add to the pan along with the white wine. Cook over a low heat until the wine has evaporated. Add the rice and continue to cook for a further 15 minutes, adding as much of the hot cooking water from the octopus as needed, a ladleful at a time, until the rice is mostly soft with just a small bite.

Meanwhile, prepare the sauce. In a bowl, mix together the ginger and garlic with 50ml (2fl oz) of the olive oil and the lemon zest. Season with salt and pepper.

Preheat the grill or a frying pan until hot. Drizzle the rest of the octopus with 3 tablespoons of the olive oil and grill or fry until brown on all sides.

Stir two-thirds of the ginger sauce into the risotto to thicken it. Add the lemon juice, the remaining 2 tablespoons of olive oil, parsley and fennel fronds and stir to combine. Serve the risotto topped with the grilled/fried octopus and the remaining ginger sauce on the side.

Tip

If you are struggling to source black (Venere) rice, you could add squid ink (easily found in Italian delis or at the fishmonger) to Carnaroli rice. Just reduce the initial 30 minutes of cooking time to around 20 minutes.

Accompany with a Carricante Bianco or another Sicilian white wine.

A word on risottos and couscous

Cùscusu (in the local dialect) is the typical version of couscous in Sicily, made with fish. It arrived on the island during the Arab occupation, 827–1061 CE, and is a speciality of the Trapani region. Originally, it was a poor man's meal, prepared by fishermen, but today, depending on the type of fish used, it is a much more up-market dish. I invite you to discover this couscous for yourself by eating it at San Vito Lo Capo, one of the beautiful seaside villages on the northwest coast not far from Trapani, where a fish couscous festival is held every September.

As for risotto, which might be considered a speciality of northern Italy, in recent years it has been a regular feature in Sicily, made primarily with fish or vegetables.

Lobster risotto
Risotto all'astice

Lobster risotto is a gorgeous dish to serve during the festive season. Ideally, use fresh lobster or crayfish, but both are available frozen, which is the more affordable option, and that is what I've used for this recipe.

Preparation time: 20 minutes
Defrosting time: 1 hour
Cooking time: 1 hour 30 minutes
Serves 4

- 2 × 600g (1lb 5oz) frozen ready-cooked lobsters
- 150g (5½oz) raw langoustines
- 120–135ml (4–4¾fl oz) olive oil, plus extra for drizzling
- 2 garlic cloves, sliced into short sticks
- 2 small leeks, white parts only
- 1 teaspoon thyme leaves
- 1 bay leaf
- pinch of saffron threads
- 1 bird's-eye chilli
- 150ml (5fl oz) dry white wine
- 5 tomatoes, scalded and skinned
- 1 shallot, finely chopped
- 350g (12oz) Carnaroli rice
- 10g (¼oz) butter
- sea salt flakes
- snipped chives, to garnish

Take the lobsters from the freezer, unwrap and leave to defrost for 1 hour at room temperature.

Remove the lobster meat from the shells and slice thinly. Layer the sliced meat between 2 sheets of nonstick baking paper and place in the refrigerator. Peel the langoustines, cut into small pieces and refrigerate, reserving the heads and shells for making the stock.

Heat 60ml (4 tablespoons) of the olive oil in a large saucepan or stockpot over a medium heat and fry the garlic until golden. Add the leeks, the langoustine heads and shells, thyme leaves, bay leaf, saffron threads, chilli, 100ml (3½fl oz) of the wine and the tomatoes. Cook for about 5 minutes, then add 1.5 litres (3 pints) of water, cover the pan and simmer for about 1 hour, adding more water if the level drops. Strain the stock and keep hot.

Heat the remaining 60–75ml (4–5 tablespoons) of the olive oil in a large sauté pan and fry the shallot over a medium heat until golden. Add the rice and cook until it develops a pearly sheen. Pour in the remaining wine and cook over a low heat until it evaporates. Gradually add the hot stock, a ladleful at a time, allowing the rice to absorb the stock before adding the next. Cook for about 20 minutes, stirring frequently, until the rice is almost al dente. Towards the end of the cooking time, add the langoustine pieces and stir in the butter to thicken the risotto a little.

To serve, divide the risotto between 4 serving plates, spreading it in an even layer. Arrange about 6 slices of lobster on each plate, slightly overlapping, in the centre of the risotto. Lightly season the lobster 'carpaccio' with sea salt flakes and garnish with snipped chives and a drizzle of olive oil. Serve immediately.

Tips

In Sicily, grated cheese is never added to a fish risotto (nor to any pasta dish with fish).

Accompany with a white Sicilian wine, such as an Etna.

Artichoke and pea risotto
Risotto con carciofi e piselli

This dish is ideal for vegetarians – if you omit the anchovies. It is best to use the small, cone-shaped Violette artichokes, which are more tender than globe artichokes and have a better flavour.

Preparation time: 15 minutes
Cooking time: 25–30 minutes
Serves 4

- 5 Sicilian Violette artichokes or globe artichokes
- juice of 1 lemon
- 6 tablespoons olive oil
- 1 garlic clove, finely chopped
- 1 onion, finely chopped
- 4–5 anchovy fillets in olive oil
- 150g (5½oz) fresh peas
- 350g (12oz) Carnaroli rice
- 1 litre (1¾ pints) hot light vegetable stock or simmering water
- 10g (¼oz) butter
- bunch of flat-leaf parsley, chopped (optional)
- 60g (2¼oz) pecorino or Parmesan cheese
- salt and freshly ground black pepper

Trim the artichokes, keeping only the hearts and stalks. To do this, remove all the tough outer leaves, trim the tops and then remove the hairy choke with a spoon. Slice them into quarters or sixths, cutting the stalks into small pieces and set aside in a bowl of cold water to which the lemon juice has been added.

Heat the olive oil in a large sauté pan and fry the garlic and onion over a medium heat until golden. After 1–2 minutes, add the anchovies, breaking them up with a fork. Drain the artichokes and add to the pan with the peas and season with salt and pepper. Moisten with 50ml (2fl oz) of water and leave to cook over a low heat until the water evaporates. Stir in the rice, then add the hot vegetable stock or water a ladleful at a time, allowing the rice to absorb each ladleful before adding the next. Cook for about 20 minutes, stirring frequently, until the rice is al dente.

Once the rice is cooked, add the butter. Sprinkle over the chopped parsley (if using) and grated pecorino or Parmesan.

Serve immediately.

Tip

Accompany with a Cerasuolo Donnafugata Rosso or another Sicilian red wine.

Trapani couscous

Couscous trapanese

This dish is particularly close to my heart as it reminds me of my grandmother. I can picture her skinning and filleting fish (by hand, of course!), removing every last bit of skin and bone. You can ask your fishmonger to clean and fillet the fish, if you wish.

Preparation time: 15 minutes
Resting time: 30 minutes
Cooking time: 1 hour
Serves 6

- 2 pinches of saffron threads
- 600g (1lb 5oz) medium couscous (preferably the Ferrero brand)
- 300ml (10fl oz) olive oil
- 2kg (4lb 8oz) mixed whole fish (for example, gurnard, sea bass, sea bream), cleaned, prepared and filleted
- 1 onion, finely chopped
- 3 garlic cloves, finely chopped
- 2 × 400g (14oz) cans of Italian peeled tomatoes, cut into small dice
- bunch of flat-leaf parsley, chopped
- 1 bay leaf
- salt and freshly ground black pepper

To prepare the couscous, add a pinch of saffron to a small bowl with 250ml (9fl oz) of water. Tip the couscous into a large bowl and pour in the saffron water. Mix with a fork and leave for 10 minutes for the grains to swell. Add 150ml (5fl oz) of the olive oil, season with salt and pepper, and fluff up the grains with the fork. Transfer to a couscoussier (see Tip, below) and steam for 30 minutes, stirring frequently with a wooden spoon.

To prepare the *ghiotta* (fish sauce), cut the fish into large pieces. Heat the remaining oil in a large saucepan or stockpot and fry the onion and garlic over a medium heat until golden. Add the tomatoes, chopped parsley and another pinch of saffron and cook for 5 minutes over a low heat. Next, add the pieces of fish and pour in about 2–3 litres (3½–5¼ pints) water. Add the bay leaf, season with salt and pepper, cover and bring to the boil. Cook over a low heat for about 30 minutes.

Once the couscous is cooked, transfer it to a serving dish, add 2 ladlefuls of the fish sauce and mix together. Cover with foil and a tea towel and leave to rest for 20 minutes. Remove the tea towel and foil, add the fish fillets and spoon over the rest of the sauce. Serve hot.

Tips

If you do not have a couscoussier, use a pan of simmering water with a steam basket on top. Alternatively, cook the couscous according to the packet instructions and simply add 2 or 3 ladles of hot broth, as well as the fish, before serving. Dust the couscous with a pinch of cinnamon, if you wish.

You can also add some mussels and large, cooked prawns as a garnish. Heat 4 tablespoons of olive oil in a frying pan and fry 1 finely chopped garlic clove and 1 finely chopped small shallot until golden. Add 500g (1lb 2oz) washed mussels, 50ml (2fl oz) white wine and a little chopped parsley. Cook, covered, for 5 minutes, stirring once or twice. Fish out the mussels, remove from their shells and return to the sauce. Arrange the mussels and prawns on top of the couscous. Any cooking juices can be added to the fish sauce.

Serve with an Inzolia Bianco or other Sicilian white wine.

Couscous with cuttlefish, mussels and prawns

Couscous al nero di sepia, cozze e gamberi

This is a modern and more sophisticated version of a traditional dish, but just as delicious!

Preparation time: 15 minutes
Cooking time: 40 minutes
Serves 4

- 150ml (5fl oz) olive oil
- 2 shallots, chopped
- 500g (1lb 2oz) canned San Marzano peeled tomatoes, cut into small dice
- 500g (1lb 2oz) extra-large prawns, cleaned and shelled
- 2 garlic cloves, crushed
- 1.5kg (3lb 5oz) mussels
- small bunch (20 sprigs) of flat-leaf parsley, plus extra to garnish
- 200ml (7fl oz) dry white wine
- 500g (1lb 2oz) raw cuttlefish, cleaned and cut into small pieces
- 20g (¾oz) tomato purée
- 1 sachet cuttlefish ink (5–6 tablespoons)
- 500g (1lb 2oz) medium couscous (preferably the Ferrero brand)
- salt and freshly ground black pepper

Heat 45ml (3 tablespoons) of the olive oil in a sauté pan and fry the shallots over a medium heat until golden. Add the tomatoes, season with salt and pepper, stir well and cook for about 5 minutes, then add the prawns and fry for a few minutes.

In a large saucepan or stockpot, heat another 45ml (3 tablespoons) of the oil, half of the garlic, the mussels, parsley and 100ml (3½fl oz) of the wine. Once boiling, cover the pan and cook for 4–5 minutes.

Scoop out the mussels and remove from their shells. Strain the cooking liquid and reserve it. Add the mussels and half the cooking liquid to the sauté pan containing the sauce and prawns. Continue cooking over a low heat for 5 minutes.

In a separate frying pan, heat the remaining olive oil and gently fry the rest of the garlic for 5 minutes until golden. Add the cuttlefish, tomato purée, the remaining mussel cooking liquid, cuttlefish ink and the remaining wine and season with salt and pepper. If you do not have much mussel juice, add a little water instead. Cook over a low heat for 15 minutes.

Prepare the couscous in the traditional way (see page 102), or the quicker, more modern way, following the instructions on the packet. Season and transfer the couscous to a serving dish. Spoon the seafood and tomato sauce on top and serve hot, garnished with parsley sprigs.

Tips

Ask your fishmonger to collect the ink when cleaning the cuttlefish for you.

Accompany with a Grillo Bianco or another Sicilian white wine.

Meat
CARNE

Small meat pies

Pastieri di carne

These little meat pies hail from the province of Ragusa in southeast Sicily and are mainly eaten at Eastertime. They are mini volcanoes, filled with minced meat and caciocavallo – a hard cheese common throughout southern Italy – or, as I use here, Sicilian pecorino.

Preparation time: 30 minutes
Resting time: 30 minutes
Cooking time: 20 minutes
Makes 12

For the pastry:
- 350g (12oz) type '00' flour, plus extra for dusting
- 50ml (2fl oz) lukewarm water
- 1 egg, beaten
- 1 teaspoon salt
- 200ml (7fl oz) olive oil
- 2 tablespoons lemon juice

For the filling:
- 300g (10½oz) lean minced pork or lamb, or a mix of pork and veal
- 1 garlic clove, chopped
- small bunch of flat-leaf parsley, chopped, plus extra leaves to garnish
- 30g (1oz) grated Sicilian pecorino cheese
- 1 whole egg
- 1 egg yolk, beaten, for glazing
- salt and freshly ground black pepper

To prepare the pastry, sift the flour into a bowl, make a well in the centre and pour in the lukewarm water and beaten egg. Stir together with a fork. Add the salt, olive oil and lemon juice and mix to form a dough. Knead energetically until the dough is smooth and elastic. Cover it with a clean tea towel and leave to rest in a warm place for about 30 minutes.

Meanwhile, prepare the filling. Put the minced pork in a bowl with the garlic, parsley, grated pecorino and the whole egg and season with salt and pepper. Mix everything together until evenly combined.

Preheat the oven to 180°C (350°F), Gas Mark 4.

To make the pies, roll out the pastry on a lightly floured work surface until 2–3mm (1/16–1/8in) thick. Use a 12cm (4½in) cookie cutter to make 12 rounds.

Spoon a little of the filling into the centre of each pastry round. Gather up the edges to shape into small pouches, leaving them slightly open at the top. Brush the pastry with the beaten egg yolk, dabbing a few drops onto the exposed filling.

Transfer the pies to a baking sheet and bake for about 20 minutes. Serve hot, garnished with a few parsley leaves.

Tips

To save time, use readymade shortcrust pastry or pizza dough, rolled out thinly.

Accompany with an Etna Rosato sul Vulcano Donnafugata or another Sicilian rosé wine.

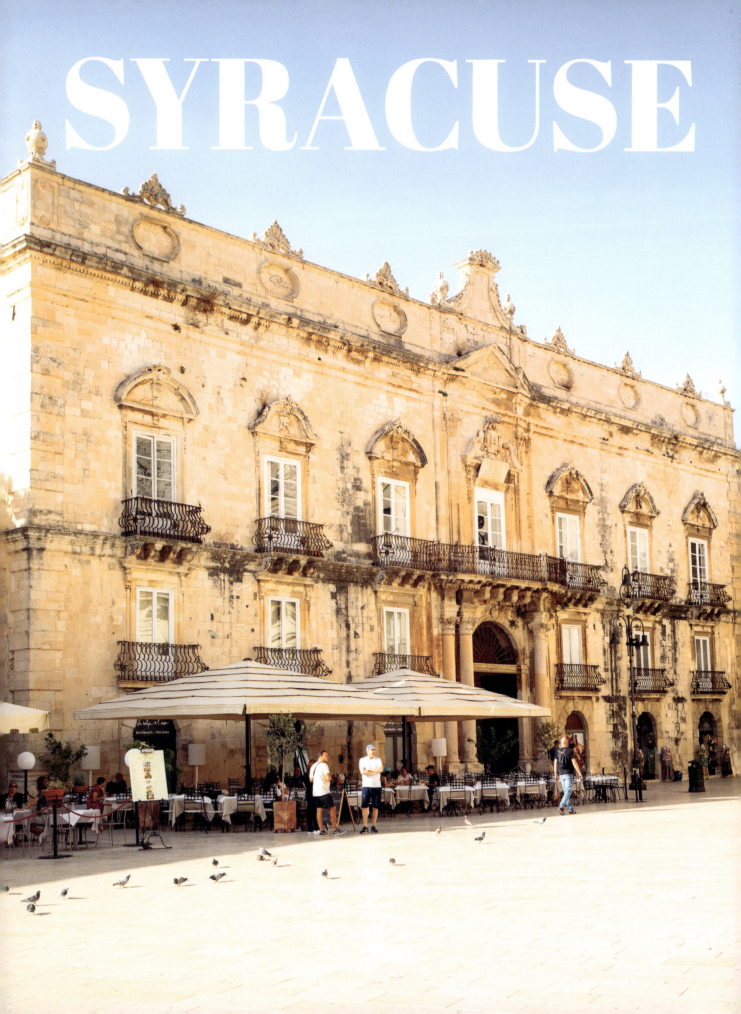

SYRACUSE

Meatloaf with vegetable sauce
Polpettone alle verdure

Meatloaf is a traditional family meal, featuring regularly on Sicilian tables. You can serve it with vegetables, as I've done here, or coated with a basil and tomato sauce (see page 52). Even cold it's still good – perfect for a picnic!

Preparation time: 20 minutes
Cooking time: 50 minutes
Serves 6

- 50g (1¾oz) sliced white bread loaf
- 100ml (3½fl oz) milk
- 500g (1lb 2oz) minced veal
- 200g (7oz) sausagemeat
- 4 eggs
- 40g (1½oz) grated Parmesan cheese
- 1 small garlic clove, chopped
- 20 flat-leaf parsley sprigs, chopped
- 40g (1½oz) dry breadcrumbs
- 1 teaspoon flour, plus extra for dusting
- 50ml (2fl oz) olive oil
- 1 small onion, finely chopped
- 1 small celery heart, cubed
- 3 carrots, cut into small dice
- 50ml (2fl oz) dry Marsala wine
- 200ml (7fl oz) vegetable stock
- juice of ½ lemon (optional)
- salt and freshly ground black pepper

Preheat the oven to 180°C (350°F), Gas Mark 4.

Soak the bread in the milk, then squeeze out the excess. Mix together the veal and sausagemeat in a large bowl, beat 3 of the eggs and add to the bowl with the soaked bread, Parmesan, garlic, parsley and dry breadcrumbs. Season well, then combine everything thoroughly and shape into a loaf.

Beat the remaining egg, brush it over the meatloaf and dust with flour. Roll up the loaf in a sheet of nonstick baking paper and then wrap in foil. Place in a shallow ovenproof dish and bake for around 40 minutes. Remove from the oven, unwrap and leave to cool.

Heat the oil in a flameproof casserole large enough to fit the meatloaf and fry the onion over a medium heat until golden. Add the celery and carrots and stir for 3 minutes. Deglaze with the Marsala, add the teaspoon of flour and pour in the stock. Continue to cook for about another 20 minutes.

Carefully lift the meatloaf into the casserole and cook for a further 10 minutes, basting it regularly with the sauce.

Just before serving, squeeze over the lemon juice (if using) and serve sliced, with the sauce.

Tip
Accompany with a Cerasuolo Donnafugata or another Sicilian red wine.

Nonna's glazed meat and egg roll

Braciolone agglassato della nonna

Every region has a different recipe for this very tasty Sicilian dish and, of course, every family thinks theirs is the best! Mine is certainly the most generous.

Preparation time: 30 minutes
Cooking time: 45–50 minutes
Serves 4

- 600g (1lb 5oz) veal escalope, cut into very thin slices
- 15 flat-leaf parsley sprigs, finely chopped
- 50g (1¾oz) grated Parmesan or pecorino cheese
- 8 thin slices of mortadella
- 4–5 hard-boiled eggs, shelled
- 6 tablespoons olive oil
- 1 onion, finely chopped
- 1 garlic clove
- 50ml (2fl oz) dry Marsala wine
- 700ml (1¼ pints) passata
- 10 basil leaves or 2 tablespoons chopped fresh basil
- 500g (1lb 2oz) frozen peas
- 2 teaspoons sugar
- 300ml (10fl oz) vegetable stock
- salt and freshly ground black pepper

Flatten the veal slices by placing them between 2 sheets of baking paper and hitting them with a rolling pin. Arrange the slices in a line, overlapping them so that they can be rolled around the filling. Season with salt and pepper, and scatter the parsley and Parmesan over them. Top with the mortadella slices and sit the whole hard-boiled eggs in a line down the centre. Wrap the veal around the mortadella and eggs, to form a large roll. Use kitchen string to tie the roll so that it keeps its shape during cooking.

Heat the olive oil in a large flameproof casserole over a medium heat and fry the onion and whole garlic clove until golden. Add the meat and egg roll and brown it on all sides, basting it with the oil. Add the Marsala, passata, basil, peas, sugar and vegetable stock so that the roll is covered. Season with salt and pepper and leave to simmer over a gentle heat for around 40 minutes, half-covering the casserole with a lid.

Lift the roll out of the casserole and remove the string. Remove the garlic clove from the sauce, then slice the roll and serve it hot with the sauce.

Tips

Serve the roll with fresh tagliatelle.

Accompany with a Rapitalà Rosso or another Sicilian red wine.

Pork stew
Stufato di maiale

This is a dish for Sunday lunch, especially if served with Ravioli (see page 84). The fennel sausages enhance the flavour of the tomato sauce and the sweetness of the ricotta. To aid digestion, I'd suggest a nice lemon ice cream for dessert, followed by a long afternoon siesta!

Preparation time: 10 minutes
Cooking time: 1 hour 40 minutes
Serves 4

- 4 fresh pork and fennel sausages (available in Italian delicatessens)
- 150ml (5fl oz) olive oil
- 2 large garlic cloves
- about 150g (5½oz) Parma ham rind (see Tip, below), cut into small pieces
- 2 thick slices (the equivalent of 3 fingers) lean shoulder of pork, cut into bite-size pieces
- 700ml (1¼ pints) passata
- 280g (10oz) frozen petits pois
- 700ml (1¼ pints) cold water
- 5 teaspoons sugar
- 6 large basil leaves or 2 tablespoons chopped fresh basil
- salt and freshly ground black pepper

Prick the sausages and blanch them for 3 minutes in a saucepan of boiling water, then drain.

Heat the oil in a cast-iron casserole over a medium heat and fry the garlic cloves and Parma ham rind until golden. Chop the sausages and add to the casserole with the pieces of pork and fry until browned.

Stir in the passata, peas, water, sugar and basil, half-cover the casserole with a lid and leave to simmer for about 1–1½ hours, or until the sauce has thickened, checking and stirring it frequently.

Remove the garlic cloves, then serve immediately.

Tip

Parma ham rind can be bought from your butcher.

Accompany with a Nero d'Avola Rosato or another Sicilian rosé wine.

Meatballs au naturel
Polpette in bianco

This dish is a favourite with children, served on its own or with a tomato sauce and accompanied by pasta. If you make the meatballs using a mix of different meats (half veal, half pork), they will be softer. In summer, I like to serve them cold with *peperonata* (see Tip) spooned over. Feel free to add fresh herbs, such as parsley or basil.

Preparation time: 10 minutes
Cooking time: 35–40 minutes
Serves 4

- 500g (1lb 2oz) minced beef
- 2 eggs, beaten
- 40g (1½oz) sliced white bread loaf
- 80ml (2¾fl oz) milk
- 1 garlic clove, chopped
- 15 flat-leaf parsley sprigs, chopped
- 80g (2¾oz) grated Parmesan cheese
- 2–3 tablespoons dry breadcrumbs
- flour, for dusting
- olive oil, for frying
- 1 onion, chopped
- 500ml (18fl oz) beef stock
- salt and freshly ground black pepper

Put the minced beef in a mixing bowl and add the eggs. Soak the bread in the milk, squeeze out the excess, then crumble it into the mixing bowl. Add the garlic, parsley, grated Parmesan and dry breadcrumbs and season with salt and pepper. Mix everything thoroughly together, shape it into small balls and dust with flour.

Heat a little olive oil in a frying pan over a medium heat, add the onion and meatballs and fry until the onion and meatballs are golden brown. Add the beef stock and continue to cook for around 30 minutes over a very gentle heat.

Leave to cool a little before serving with salad alongside or *peperonata* spooned over the meatballs.

Tips

Peperonata is simply a mix of red peppers, onions, tomatoes, basil, salt and freshly ground black pepper, gently fried together until soft, with red wine vinegar added at the end of cooking to deglaze the pan.

Accompany with a Rosato di Nerello Mascalese or another Sicilian rosé wine.

Veal escalopes and ham served pizza-style
Carne alla pizzaiola

A recipe that combines breaded veal escalopes and pizza toppings. It's a richly flavoured dish that is popular with children, and with adults too – like me! It's very tasty and I love it.

Preparation time: 10 minutes
Marinating time: 1 hour
Cooking time 25 minutes
Serves 4

- 800g (1lb 12oz) very thin veal escalopes
- 2 eggs
- 100g (3½oz) dry breadcrumbs
- 15–30ml (1–2 tablespoons) olive oil, plus extra for greasing
- 500g (1lb 2oz) canned chopped tomatoes
- a few very thin slices of cooked ham
- 80g (2¾oz) grated Parmesan cheese
- 2 tablespoons dried oregano
- 250g (9oz) cows' milk mozzarella cheese, thinly sliced
- salt and freshly ground black pepper

If the escalopes are very large, cut them into 2 or 3 pieces (roughly 7–8cm/2¾–3¼in).

Beat the eggs with some salt and pepper in a large shallow dish, add the veal escalopes and leave them to marinate for 1 hour in the refrigerator.

Preheat the oven to 180°C (350°F), Gas Mark 4. Grease a large shallow ovenproof dish with olive oil.

Lift the escalopes out of the beaten egg and coat them in the breadcrumbs. Arrange in a single layer in the dish. Pour over the chopped tomatoes, and lay the ham slices on top. Sprinkle over the grated Parmesan and most of the oregano. Drizzle with the olive oil according to your preference and bake for about 20 minutes.

Remove from the oven and lay the mozzarella slices on top. Sprinkle over the remaining oregano and return to the oven for at least 5 minutes to melt the mozzarella. Serve hot.

Tip
Accompany with a Rosato di Nerello Mascalese or another Sicilian rosé wine.

Fish

PESCE

Oven-baked turbot with bottarga

Rombo al forno alla bottarga

Turbot, a noble fish, is baked with fragrant produce from Sicily – capers, olives and tomatoes – plus the added aroma of oregano, the herb that is an essential part of the island's cuisine. This is a sophisticated dish, enhanced by the addition of thinly sliced bottarga.

Preparation time: 10 minutes
Cooking time: 12 minutes
Serves 4

- 2 garlic cloves, one whole, one chopped
- 100ml (3½fl oz) olive oil
- 800g (1lb 12oz) turbot fillets, skin on
- 100g (3½oz) Taggiasche black olives, pitted
- 50g (1¾oz) capers in salt, soaked then rinsed
- 1 teaspoon dried oregano
- leaves from a few myrtle sprigs (optional)
- 1 small fresh chilli, very finely chopped
- pinch of salt
- 12 cherry tomatoes, halved
- 5 tablespoons dry white wine
- 70g (2½oz) grey mullet bottarga

Line a large shallow baking dish with nonstick baking paper and rub with the whole garlic clove. Brush with about 60ml (4 tablespoons) of the olive oil and lay the turbot fillets on top, skin-side down.

Preheat the oven to 180°C (350°F), Gas Mark 4.

Add the chopped garlic to a bowl with the olives, capers, oregano, myrtle (if using) and chilli. Pour in the remaining olive oil and a pinch of salt. Mix well to make a sauce.

Pour the sauce over the fish fillets, add the halved cherry tomatoes and wine. Bake for about 12 minutes.

As soon as you remove the fish from the oven, thinly slice the bottarga and divide the slices between the fillets. Serve immediately.

Tip

Serve with a Catarratto Bianco or another Sicilian white wine.

Braised salt cod
Baccalà in umido

The origins of this dish go back a very long way and traditionally it is eaten on religious holidays before Easter. It's easy to make, and the ingredients deliver huge flavour – you just need to find some very good salt cod!

Preparation: 10 minutes
Cooking: 1 hour 20 minutes
Serves 4

- 100ml (3½fl oz) olive oil
- 1 garlic clove
- 1 onion, finely chopped
- 300g (10½oz) canned chopped tomatoes
- 30g (1oz) capers in vinegar
- 2 tablespoons pine nuts
- 2 tablespoons raisins
- 100g (3½oz) green olives, pitted
- 500g (1lb 2oz) potatoes, peeled and cut into large chunks
- 1kg (2lb 4oz) salt cod fillets, desalted (see Tip, page 16)
- 100g (3½oz) flour
- 150ml (5fl oz) grapeseed oil
- 50ml (2fl oz) dry white wine
- small bunch of flat-leaf parsley, chopped
- salt

Heat the olive oil in a large frying pan over a medium heat and fry the whole garlic clove with the chopped onion until golden. Remove the garlic from the pan and add the chopped tomatoes, capers, pine nuts, raisins and olives. Stir everything together, add 75ml (2½fl oz) water and cook over a low heat for about 10 minutes to cook the tomatoes a little. Add the potatoes and cook for another 10 minutes.

Dust the salt cod fillets with the flour and fry them in batches in the grapeseed oil in a separate large frying pan. Deglaze the pan with the white wine, then transfer the contents to the tomato sauce.

Continue to cook for about 20 minutes over a low heat, adding a little water and seasoning with salt if needed. Sprinkle over the chopped parsley and serve hot.

Tip

Accompany this dish with a Rosato di Nerello Mascalese or another Sicilian rosé wine.

Sweet-and-sour sea bass carpaccio
Ricciola in agrodolce

In Sicily, a fish called *ricciola* (amberjack) would be used to make this dish, but it's not widely available elsewhere. Therefore, I use sea bass, which is easy to source and very similar to *ricciola* – just as lean and rich in protein. The fish has to be extremely fresh, so let your fishmonger know you are making carpaccio. The pistachio and basil pesto, along with the marinade, boost the flavour of the fish and, as in other recipes, the dried fruit adds both crunch and a Sicilian touch.

Preparation time: 20 minutes
Marinating time: 15 minutes
Serves 4

- 25g (1oz) pistachios, shelled
- 30 basil leaves
- 1 small garlic clove, crushed
- about 8 tablespoons olive oil
- 3 tablespoons white wine vinegar
- 1 level tablespoon brown sugar
- 500g (1lb 2oz) skinless sea bass fillets (see Tip, below), rinsed and dried
- 30g (1oz) pine nuts
- 40g (1½oz) raisins
- a few curly endive salad leaves
- salt and freshly ground black pepper

Grind the pistachios and basil leaves together to a paste in a food processor. Transfer the paste to a bowl, add the garlic, season with a pinch of salt and freshly ground black pepper and add enough of the olive oil to make a pesto. Set aside.

Gently heat the vinegar in a small pan, add the sugar and leave until the sugar dissolves. Remove from the heat and leave to cool.

Check the sea bass for any bones and thinly slice the fillets. Place in a shallow dish, pour over the vinegar and sugar, season with salt and pepper, cover with clingfilm and leave to marinate in the refrigerator for about 15 minutes.

Meanwhile, toast the pine nuts and raisins in a dry frying pan.

Arrange a bed of salad leaves on each serving plate, drain the fish fillets from the marinade and place them on top. Garnish with the pine nuts and raisins and spoon over the pistachio pesto. Serve immediately.

Tip

If using wild fish, prepare it beforehand by freezing it for a minimum of 24 hours to ensure no bacteria is present, then allow it to defrost in the fridge. There is no need to freeze farmed fish, but I suggest putting it in the freezer for 1 hour before use so it is easier to slice.

Accompany with a Piano Maltese Bianco or another Sicilian white wine.

Beer-battered salt cod
Baccalà fritto

Deep-frying chunks of cod in batter until crisp is a simple and effective way to cook fish and possibly the only way you can persuade children to eat it, especially if chips are on the side! Personally, I like to serve this with *Caponata* (see page 39) or *peperonata* (see Tip, page 122).

Preparation time: 15 minutes
Resting time: 20 minutes
Cooking time: 6 minutes
Serves 4

- 130g (4½oz) plain flour
- 1 egg, separated
- 1 tablespoon grapeseed oil
- 200ml (7fl oz) blonde beer
- 500g (1lb 2oz) salt cod fillets, desalted (see Tip, page 16) and skinned
- oil, for deep-frying
- salt and freshly ground black pepper

First, prepare the batter. Sift the flour into a mixing bowl and make a well in the centre. Add the egg yolk to the well along with the grapeseed oil, a pinch of salt and some freshly ground pepper. Gradually whisk in enough beer, a little at a time, to form a thin, creamy batter. Cover the bowl and leave the batter to rest for about 20 minutes.

Whisk the egg white with a pinch of salt until stiff peaks form, then fold into the batter.

Heat enough oil for deep-frying in a deep-sided saucepan to 180–190°C (350–375°F), or until a cube of bread browns in 30 seconds.

Cut the salt cod into cubes and dip them first in batter to coat completely, then add them to the hot oil. Fry in batches until a deep golden brown. Drain on a plate lined with kitchen paper and serve them hot to nibble with an aperitif or with chips and a salad.

Variation

Put the freshly fried salt cod cubes in an ovenproof dish and cover with tomato sauce *alla puttanesca* (made with 3-4 peeled and chopped tomatoes or 250ml (9fl oz) passata, garlic, olive oil, anchovies, capers, olives, parsley and oregano). Place in an oven preheated to 160°C (325°F), Gas Mark 3 for 5-8 minutes until hot.

Tips

In summer, you can serve this dish cold - it will be even tastier!

Accompany with a Rapitalà Bianco or another Sicilian white wine.

Tuna carpaccio
Millefoglie di tonno

To make this carpaccio, it is essential to buy the freshest possible tuna, so speak to your fishmonger. The sauce, based on olive oil, chives, oregano and almonds, does the rest!

Preparation time: 10 minutes
Marinating time: 2 hours
Serves 4

- 4 firm tomatoes, sliced
- juice of 2 lemons
- 200g (7oz) tuna fillet (see Tip, page 134), sliced very thinly for carpaccio
- 50ml (2fl oz) olive oil, plus a drizzle for the carpaccio
- 1 tablespoon chopped chives
- 1 tablespoon chopped oregano
- 30g (1oz) almonds, roughly chopped
- salt and freshly ground black pepper

Season the tomatoes with salt and pepper, and leave to drain on a sheet of nonstick baking paper.

Meanwhile, put the tuna in a shallow dish and squeeze two-thirds of the lemon juice over the slices and add a generous drizzle of olive oil. Marinate for 2 hours in the refrigerator.

To prepare the sauce, put the chopped chives, oregano and almonds in a bowl. Cover with the 50ml (2fl oz) of olive oil, season with salt and pepper and add the rest of the lemon juice. Mix all the ingredients together thoroughly.

Assemble alternate layers of tomato and tuna slices on 4 serving plates and spoon the sauce over. Serve well chilled.

Tip
Accompany with an Inzolia Bianco or another Sicilian white wine.

Sardine tartlets
Tortini di sarde

The name of this recipe derives from its shape, which resembles a small tart or pie. As you will see from how to make it, however, no pie crust is involved. It's a dish that's not too expensive to make but tastes really good.

Preparation time: 15 minutes
Cooking time: 6 minutes
Serves 4

- 1 garlic clove, chopped
- 20 flat-leaf parsley sprigs, chopped
- 20 basil leaves, chopped, plus extra leaves to garnish
- 24 fresh sardines, cleaned, heads and tails removed, filleted and laid flat, skin-side down
- 4 beef tomato slices, 1cm (½in) thick
- 4 tablespoons grated Parmesan cheese
- 4 tablespoons dry breadcrumbs
- 50ml (2fl oz) Sicilian olive oil, plus extra for drizzling
- salt and freshly ground black pepper

To prepare the filling, mix together the chopped garlic, parsley and basil. Season the inside of the sardines with salt and pepper and spoon the herb mixture into the centre of each. Close and reshape the sardines.

Season the tomato slices with salt and pepper and leave to drain on a sheet of nonstick baking paper.

Preheat the oven to 200°C (400°F), Gas Mark 6.

Place 4 metal moulds, each 6–8cm (2½–3¼in) in diameter, on a baking sheet lined with nonstick baking paper and put 3 stuffed sardines in a single layer in each. Season with salt and pepper, sprinkle with half of the grated Parmesan and cover with a tomato slice. Top with 3 more stuffed sardines, 1 tablespoon of dry breadcrumbs, the remaining grated Parmesan and add a generous drizzle of olive oil to each mould. Bake for 6 minutes.

Carefully transfer the tartlets to serving plates and unmould. Serve garnished with a few basil leaves and drizzle over a little Sicilian olive oil in celebration of the Mediterranean flavours of sardines, fresh herbs and tomatoes. Serve immediately.

Tip
Accompany with a Grecanico Bianco or another Sicilian white wine.

Hearty octopus soup
Ghiotta di polpo

Octopus appears in numerous Sicilian recipes, from salads and pasta dishes to risotto. In this recipe I'm using rock octopus, which is small and full of flavour.

Preparation: 20 minutes
Cooking: 1 hour
Serves 4

- 1.2kg (2lb 12oz) rock octopus (or any octopus from your fishmonger), preferably frozen then defrosted
- 100ml (3½fl oz) olive oil
- 2 shallots, finely chopped
- 4 garlic cloves, chopped
- 2 thyme sprigs
- 1 bay leaf
- 400ml (14fl oz) cold water
- 100ml (3½fl oz) dry white wine
- 400g (14oz) passata or canned chopped tomatoes
- large pinch of saffron threads
- pared rind of ½ orange
- salt and freshly ground black pepper
- 1 French stick (small baguette) cut into thin slices, toasted, to serve

For the spicy mayonnaise:
- 2 egg yolks
- 2 garlic cloves, chopped
- 1 teaspoon mustard
- pinch of sweet paprika
- pinch of saffron
- 150ml (5fl oz) olive oil

Wash the octopus, pat dry with kitchen paper and cut into small pieces.

Heat 50ml (2fl oz) of the olive oil in a flameproof casserole over a medium heat and fry the shallots, half of the garlic, the thyme and bay leaf until the shallots are golden. Add the octopus and 200ml (7fl oz) of the measured water, cover the pan and cook over a low heat for 20 minutes. Add the wine, passata or chopped tomatoes, a pinch of saffron threads and the orange rind and season with salt and pepper. Pour in the remaining 200ml (7fl oz) of water, cover the pan again and leave to simmer for 30 minutes over a low heat.

Meanwhile, prepare the spicy mayonnaise. Whisk the egg yolks, garlic, mustard, paprika, saffron and salt together. Drizzle in the olive oil, little by little, whisking all the while – the mayonnaise should be very thick and creamy. Refrigerate for 30 minutes before serving.

Toast the bread slices. Remove the thyme sprigs, bay leaf and orange rind from the soup and serve it with the toasted bread slices spread with the spicy mayonnaise and dipped into it.

Tips

I recommend using defrosted frozen octopus as it will be more tender. You can also replace the octopus with monkfish, cooking it for 15-20 minutes in total.

Accompany with an Etna Bianco or another Sicilian white wine.

Stuffed squid
Calamari ripieni

Squid are often stuffed with meat, but in this version my filling includes dried fruits – an essential ingredient in my opinion! As the recipe takes a while to prepare, I suggest you stuff the squid tubes the day before and keep them in the refrigerator, ready to cook the next day. They are a real treat!

Preparation time: 40 minutes
Cooking time: 1 hour
Serves 4

- 800g (1lb 12oz) squid (or 8 squid), cleaned and prepared
- 100ml (3½fl oz) olive oil
- 1 garlic clove, chopped
- 225ml (8fl oz) dry white wine
- 100g (3½oz) spinach leaves, washed
- 60g (2¼oz) fresh breadcrumbs
- 100ml (3½fl oz) milk
- 1 egg
- 100g (3½oz) mortadella (1 thick slice), chopped into small pieces
- 50g (1¾oz) grated Parmesan cheese
- 20g (¾oz) raisins
- 20g (¾oz) pine nuts
- 2 tablespoons chopped fresh oregano
- dry breadcrumbs (if needed)
- 1 small onion, finely diced
- 1 carrot, finely diced
- 1 celery stick, finely diced
- 500g (1lb 2oz) canned chopped tomatoes
- 10 basil leaves
- 1 tablespoon sugar
- salt and freshly ground black pepper

Rinse the squid and dry with kitchen paper. Remove the tentacles and finely chop half of them (reserving the other half).

Heat half of the olive oil in a frying pan over a medium heat and fry the garlic and chopped tentacles until the garlic is golden. Add 125ml (4fl oz) of the wine and leave to bubble until it evaporates. Remove the pan from the heat and set aside.

Heat 1 tablespoon of the olive oil in another frying pan and cook the washed spinach in the water remaining on its leaves for about 5 minutes, then drain and chop the leaves. Meanwhile, soak the fresh breadcrumbs in the milk, then squeeze out the excess liquid.

Transfer the cooked tentacles and garlic to a bowl, add the egg, mortadella, grated Parmesan, soaked breadcrumbs, raisins, pine nuts, spinach and oregano and season with salt and pepper. Mix everything together until evenly combined (add some dry breadcrumbs, if needed, to give the stuffing a good consistency).

Using a teaspoon, fill the squid tubes with the stuffing, pushing it right to the bottom. Secure the filling by closing the tubes with toothpicks.

Heat the remaining olive oil in a large sauté pan over a medium heat and fry the onion, carrot and celery until softened. Place the stuffed squid in the pan and brown on all sides over a low heat. Add the remaining tentacles, deglaze with the remaining 100ml (3½fl oz) of wine and stir until the wine has evaporated. Add the chopped tomatoes, basil, sugar and 75ml (2½fl oz) of water. Season with salt and pepper and simmer for about 30 minutes over a low heat, adding a little more water if necessary.

Tips

Sicily is brimming with small fishing ports where you can buy fish direct from the fishermen. Supreme among their bounty are swordfish and tuna, which can be served sliced, grilled, with Pachino tomatoes (cherry tomatoes), olives, capers, almonds and a citrus marinade. Their taste is exceptional – the freshness of the fish makes all the difference.

Accompany the stuffed squid with a Catarratto Bianco or another Sicilian white wine.

Swordfish with capers and almonds

Spada con capperi e mandorle

This is a classic among the island's seafood recipes. In Sicily's fish markets, swordfish (along with tuna) is a king among fish: the fishermen even recite salutations or poems about them! I know I've said this before, but the texture and freshness of swordfish you buy there makes it exceptional, and here the addition of capers, olives, oregano and almonds is guaranteed to excite your taste buds!

Preparation time: 10 minutes
Cooking time: 10–12 minutes
Serves 4

- 6 tablespoons olive oil
- 1 onion, finely chopped
- 4 swordfish steaks, 2cm (¾in) thick
- 150ml (5fl oz) dry white wine
- 10 cherry tomatoes, halved
- about 15 green olives
- 2 tablespoons capers in salt, soaked to remove the salt
- about 15 almonds, shelled
- 20g (¾oz) fresh oregano, chopped
- 2 thyme sprigs
- salt and freshly ground black pepper

Heat the olive oil in a frying pan over a medium heat and fry the onion until lightly browned. Add the swordfish steaks and fry for 1 minute on each side over a high heat until just coloured around the edges. Add the wine, halved cherry tomatoes, olives, capers and almonds and season with salt, freshly ground pepper and the oregano. Cover and leave to cook for 5–8 minutes over a low heat. Break the thyme into smaller sprigs, scatter over the fish, and serve.

Tip

Accompany with a Sicilia Menfi Chardonnay or another Sicilian white wine.

Mackerel with orange pesto

Sgombri al pesto di arancia

Mackerel is an inexpensive fish and, marinated in Sicilian citrus juice, it makes a healthy and tasty dish that is easy to prepare.

Preparation time: 15 minutes
Marinating time: 2 hours
Cooking time: 15–20 minutes
Serves 4

- 4 small blood oranges, peeled and segmented, plus extra for baking
- 200g (7oz) raw pistachios, shelled and skinned
- 50g (1¾oz) capers in salt, soaked to remove the salt
- small bunch of basil
- 100ml (3½ fl oz) olive oil
- 4 fresh mackerel, about 250g (9oz) each, cleaned, scaled but left whole
- salt and freshly ground black pepper

First, prepare the pesto. Cut the orange segments into small pieces and blend with the pistachios, capers and basil in a food processor. Add 75ml (2½fl oz) of the olive oil, a pinch of salt and freshly ground black pepper and blend again.

Place the mackerel side by side in a shallow dish and spoon over the orange pesto to cover them. Cover the dish with clingfilm and marinate in the refrigerator for 2 hours.

Preheat the oven to 180°C (350°F), Gas Mark 4 and line a baking dish with nonstick baking paper.

Spoon the pesto off the fish into a bowl and lift the drained mackerel into the baking dish. Spoon half of the pesto back over the mackerel and tuck the extra orange segments around them. Drizzle over the remaining olive oil and bake for 15–20 minutes. Serve hot with the remaining pesto.

Tip

Rather than serve the mackerel hot as soon as it is cooked, I remove the heads, tails and bones and pour the remaining pesto over the remaining fillets as I prefer to eat the dish cold the next day.

Accompany with a Grecanico Bianco or other Sicilian white wine.

Desserts

DOLCI

Sicilian cannoli
Cannoli siciliani

Once again, every family has its own recipe for making cannoli, but nobody will tell you exactly what it is, just as no one will be able to resist these crispy, golden pastry rolls, filled with creamy ricotta and flavoured with candied orange peel and chocolate shavings.

Preparation time: 30 minutes
Cooking time: 30 minutes
Makes about 20

- toasted pistachios, finely chopped, to decorate
- 30g (1oz) icing sugar, for dusting

For the pastry rolls:
- 4 eggs
- 2 tablespoons vegetable oil
- 1 teaspoon Marsala wine (optional)
- 500g (1lb 2oz) type '00' flour, plus extra for dusting
- oil, for deep-frying

For the cream filling:
- 800g (1lb 12oz) ricotta
- 1 sachet (8g/¼oz) of vanilla sugar
- 400g (14oz) caster sugar
- 2 tablespoons Maraschino cherry liqueur
- 100g (3½oz) glacé fruits or candied orange peel, plus extra to decorate
- 50g (1¾oz) plain dark chocolate, coarsely grated

First, prepare the dough for the pastry rolls. Lightly beat the eggs in a large bowl with the oil and Marsala (if using). Gradually add the flour, a little at a time, to make a fairly firm but smooth dough.

Roll out the dough thinly, about 4mm (⅛in) thick, on a lightly floured work surface and cut out about 20 rounds using a 9–10cm (3½–4in) cookie cutter. Roll them around metal cylinders, pressing quite firmly on the joins to seal them.

Heat enough oil for deep-frying in a large, deep-sided saucepan to 180–190°C (350–375°F), or until a cube of bread browns in 30 seconds. Gently lower in the cannoli, frying them in batches, until they are golden brown. Remove, then use tongs to carefully take the tubes off the metal cylinders. Leave to drain on kitchen paper until completely cool.

To prepare the cream filling, mix the ricotta with the vanilla and caster sugars and the Maraschino liqueur. Finely chop the glacé fruits or candied orange peel and fold in, along with the grated chocolate.

Once the cannoli tubes have completely cooled, fill them with the cream filling. Decorate the exposed filling at each end with a strip of candied orange peel or a glacé cherry, and sprinkle with finely chopped, toasted pistachios. Dust the cannoli with the icing sugar just before serving.

Tip

Accompany with a Zibibbo liquoroso or another sweet Muscat wine.

Cassatelle

This dessert is a great favourite with children and a little bit easier to make than Cannoli (see page 158). I can remember one Sunday afternoon when a bowl filled with these wonders, lovingly prepared by my mother, sat proudly on the kitchen table. When she returned from her walk, there were none left!

Preparation time: 30 minutes
Cooking time: 30 minutes
Makes about 20

- 1 × quantity pastry dough (see page 158)
- oil, for deep-frying
- 30g (1oz) icing sugar, for dusting

For the cream filling:
- 500g (1lb 2oz) ricotta
- 125g (4½oz) caster sugar
- 50g (1¾oz) candied orange peel, cut into small cubes
- 40g (1½oz) unsweetened cocoa powder

Prepare the dough following the recipe on page 158. Roll out the dough thinly, about 4mm (⅛in) thick, on a lightly floured work surface and cut out about 20 rounds using a 9–10cm (3½–4in) cookie cutter.

To make the filling, mash the ricotta in a mixing bowl with the caster sugar, then add the remaining ingredients, one after the other, mixing well.

Place a small amount of the filling (about 1 generous teaspoon) in the centre of each pastry disc and fold the dough over to make half-moons. Seal the edges together by pressing firmly with your fingers or a fork.

Heat enough oil for deep-frying in a large, deep-sided saucepan to 180–190°C (350–375°F), or until a cube of bread browns in 30 seconds. Fry the *cassatelle,* in batches, until golden brown. Drain on kitchen paper and serve warm, dusted with icing sugar.

Ricotta tart
Torta alla ricotta

This classic Sicilian sweet tart has a tangy ricotta and lemon filling. Simple but stunning!

Preparation time: 10 minutes
Resting time: 30 minutes
Cooking time: 40 minutes
Serves 6

For the pastry:
- 125g (4½oz) butter, diced and softened
- 250g (9oz) plain flour, plus extra for dusting
- 1 egg yolk
- pinch of salt
- 5–6 tablespoons caster sugar
- finely grated zest of 4 lemons
- 100ml (3½fl oz) water

For the filling:
- 500g (1lb 2oz) ricotta
- 3 eggs, separated
- 100g (3½oz) caster sugar
- finely grated zest of 2 lemons

To serve:
- whipped cream
- red summer fruits, such as strawberries
- icing sugar

To prepare the pastry, put the butter and flour in a large bowl and rub with your fingertips until the mixture resembles fine breadcrumbs. Mix in the egg yolk, salt, sugar, lemon zest and enough of the water to mix to a smooth dough. Shape the pastry into a ball, wrap in clingfilm and leave to rest for 30 minutes.

Preheat the oven to 180°C (350°F), Gas Mark 4.

To make the filling, mash the ricotta until smooth in a mixing bowl. Add the egg yolks, sugar and lemon zest to the bowl, mixing well. Whisk the egg whites until stiff peaks form and gently fold them into the ricotta mixture.

Roll out the pastry on a lightly floured work surface and use it to line a 26cm (10½in) tart tin. Line the pastry case with a sheet of nonstick baking paper and fill with baking beans. Bake blind for about 10 minutes. Take the pastry case out of the oven, remove the beans and baking paper, and fill with the ricotta mixture. Bake for a further 30 minutes at the same temperature.

Remove and allow to cool completely before serving as is, or you can decorate it with piped rosettes of whipped cream topped with red fruits and dusted lightly with icing sugar. Enjoy with coffee.

Variation

In winter, decorate with candied lemon slices.

Doughnuts
Bomboloni

These are the favourite treat for children during Carnevale in Sicily, the feasting before the fasting of Lent. You can eat them as you wish – plain, dusted with sugar, or filled with cream, chocolate or jam.

Preparation time: 30 minutes
Rising time: 2½–3½ hours
Cooking time: 10 minutes
Makes 8

- 250g (9oz) potatoes
- 25g (1oz) fresh yeast
- 4 tablespoons lukewarm milk
- 500g (1lb 2oz) type '00' flour, plus extra for dusting
- 50g (1¾oz) caster sugar
- finely grated zest of 1 unwaxed orange
- finely grated zest of 1 unwaxed lemon
- 50g (1¾oz) butter, diced and softened
- 2 tablespoons grapeseed or sunflower oil
- oil, for deep-frying
- icing sugar, for dusting
- salt, for cooking water

Cook the potatoes in a saucepan of salted boiling water until tender. Drain, then mash until completely smooth with no lumps remaining. Leave to cool completely.

Crumble the yeast into the lukewarm milk. Sift the flour into a mixing bowl, add the mashed potatoes, sugar, orange and lemon zests, butter and the yeast and milk mixture. Mix to form a dough, then knead until smooth.

Brush the dough with the grapeseed or sunflower oil, place in a clean bowl, cover with clingfilm and leave to rise in a warm place for 2–3 hours.

Knead the dough briefly, divide it into 8 equal pieces and roll into 7–8cm (2¾–3¼in) balls. Place the doughnuts on a clean tea towel dusted with flour and leave to rise again for 30 minutes.

Heat enough oil for deep-frying in a large, deep-sided saucepan to 180–190°C (350–375°F), or until a cube of bread browns in 30 seconds. Fry the doughnuts, in batches, until golden brown. Drain them on kitchen paper and dust with icing sugar. Eat warm.

Sicilian cassata
Cassata siciliana

The queen of Sicilian desserts, cassata first appeared during the time of the Arab occupation, sometime between the 9th and the 11th centuries. Covered with a layer of almond paste, it is eaten during the Easter holiday.

Preparation time: 40 minutes
Cooking time: 20 minutes
Serves 6

- 200g (7oz) almond paste, coloured green
- a few glacé cherries and other candied fruits, to decorate

For the sponge:
- 6 eggs, separated
- pinch of salt
- 1 level tablespoon icing sugar
- 175g (6oz) caster sugar
- 175g (6oz) type '00' flour
- 1 sachet (8g/¼oz) vanilla sugar
- finely grated zest of 1 unwaxed lemon
- knob of butter, for greasing

For the ricotta cream:
- 500–600g (1lb 2oz–1lb 5oz) ricotta
- 1 sachet (8g/¼oz) vanilla sugar
- 200g (7oz) caster sugar, plus an extra tablespoon
- 100g (3½oz) candied fruits, chopped
- 100g (3½oz) plain dark chocolate, 70% cocoa solids, shaved into curls
- 8 tablespoons Marsala Cremovo (see Tip)

To prepare the sponge cake, preheat the oven to 180°C (350°F), Gas Mark 4. Whisk the egg whites in a large bowl with the salt and icing sugar until stiff peaks form. In a separate bowl, whisk together the egg yolks and caster sugar until creamy, mousse-like and doubled in volume. Gradually fold in the flour, a little at a time, followed by the vanilla sugar and lemon zest. Fold in the whites, adding them in stages, using a spatula so as not to deflate them.

Generously grease a 26cm (10½in) cake tin with the butter, pour in the cake batter and bake for about 20 minutes (watch it carefully in case it browns too quickly). Leave to cool in the tin.

To prepare the ricotta cream, mix the ricotta with the vanilla and caster sugars, add the chopped candied fruits, the chocolate and 4 tablespoons of the Marsala Cremovo.

Bring 150ml (5fl oz) of water to the boil in a small pan with a tablespoon of sugar, and the remaining 4 tablespoons of Marsala Cremovo. Cut the sponge into 2 or 3 layers, depending on how deep the cake is, prick the layers with a skewer and spoon the liqueur syrup over them. Spread each layer with some of the ricotta cream and reassemble the cake.

Roll out the green almond paste thinly and use it to entirely cover the top and sides of the cassata. Spread more ricotta cream over the top and sides and pipe any remaining around the base of the cake. Decorate with glacé cherries and pieces of candied fruits. Chill in the refrigerator until ready to serve.

Tips

If you prepare and bake the sponge cake the day before, it will firm up and be easier to slice.

Marsala Cremovo is Marsala wine enriched with egg yolks and is a popular choice for desserts. If you can't find it, use Maraschino cherry liqueur, Grand Marnier or other liqueur.

Nonna Lucia's sweet fritters

Carteddhate di nonna Lucia

These little fritters, flavoured with orange and honey, are very popular in southern Italy where they are served during the Christmas celebrations. These are my mother's version.

Preparation time: 10 minutes
Resting time: 30 minutes
Cooking time: 30 minutes
Makes about 32

- 4 eggs
- 2 tablespoons grapeseed or sunflower oil
- 500g (1lb 2oz) type '00' flour, plus extra for dusting
- finely grated zest of 1 unwaxed orange (or 2 tablespoons orange flower water)
- pinch of salt
- oil, for deep-frying
- 500g (1lb 2oz) honey

Mix the eggs and oil together in a mixing bowl. Gradually whisk in the flour, a little at a time, with the orange zest and salt. Knead to form a smooth dough. Wrap the dough in clingfilm and leave it to rest for 30 minutes.

Roll out the dough thinly on a lightly floured work surface and, using a pasta wheel, cut it into strips 5cm (2in) wide and 10–15cm (4–6in) long.

Heat the honey in a pan and set aside.

Heat enough oil for deep-frying in a large, deep-sided saucepan to 180–190°C (350–375°F), or until a cube of bread browns in 30 seconds.

Wrap the dough strips around your hand and drop them carefully into the hot oil. Fry, in batches, until they are a rich golden brown. Drain the fritters on kitchen paper as they come out of the pan and dip them in the hot honey. Leave to cool before eating.

Tip

When making this recipe, I prepare a caramel using 250g (9oz) sugar and 2 lemons cut into very small pieces. To this, I add 100ml (3½fl oz) hot water and leave it to reduce for 10 minutes. I then add 200g (7oz) of Zagara honey (Sicilian citrus blossom honey) and soak the fritters in this hot mixture. Delicious!

A word on desserts

Sicily is also a land of sweet things! The recipes for its famous pastries are mainly based on Avola almonds, Bronte pistachios, Zagara (citrus blossom) honey and Modica chocolate. Ricotta, Sicily's must-have cheese, is used for both sweet and savoury fillings, its flavour and texture making it unique. Citrus fruits, such as lemons and oranges, grow in abundance on the island and are widely used – in particular their juice and zest – to flavour granitas and ice creams. One of the specialities of western Sicily is jasmine ice cream. Like most Sicilians, I only eat it during the summer months... but at any time of the day!

I recommend accompanying your desserts with a Sicilian sweet wine, such as a Moscato di Pantelleria, Zibibbo liquoroso, a late-harvest Malvasia delle Lipari passito, or a local *digestif,* such as a dry Grappa di passito di Pantelleria, Limoncello di Sicilia or an Amaro Averna.

Soft almond biscuits
Dolcetti di mandorle

In northern Italy, these biscuits are called amaretti and are eaten mainly at Christmastime. In Sicily, they are known as *dolcetti di mandorle* and are sold all year round in every pastry shop, but it is great fun to make them yourself at home!

Preparation time: 20 minutes
Resting time: overnight
Cooking time: 12 minutes
Makes 20 biscuits

- 1 tablespoon honey
- 100ml (3½fl oz) warm milk
- 4 egg whites
- 500g (1lb 2oz) ground almonds (see Tip)
- finely grated zest of 1 unwaxed lemon
- glacé cherries, whole blanched almonds or pieces of glacé orange peel

To decorate:
- icing sugar, for dusting
- glacé cherries (optional)

The day before, mix together the honey and warm milk. Whisk the egg whites until stiff peaks form and add to the honey and milk mixture with the ground almonds and lemon zest. Mix well, then knead to make a smooth dough.

Shape the dough into balls the size of a small walnut, flatten them slightly and place them side by side on a baking sheet lined with nonstick baking paper. Place a glacé cherry, a whole almond or some glacé orange peel in the centre of each biscuit, pressing it down lightly so it stays in place during baking.

Leave to rest overnight in the refrigerator.

The next day, preheat the oven to 180°C (350°F), Gas Mark 4. Bake the biscuits for 12 minutes.

Serve at the end of a meal, dusted liberally with icing sugar and decorated with extra glacé cherries (if using).

Tip

You can also use 250g (9oz) of ground pistachios and 250g (9oz) of ground almonds – the pistachios will tint the biscuits a pretty green colour.

Serve with a very good passito di Lipari or another Sicilian dessert wine.

Blancmange
Biancomangiare

Blancmange is a dessert that dates back to the 12th century. It has since spread from its place of origin, Arabia, throughout the Mediterranean.

Preparation time: 10 minutes
Chilling time: 6 hours
Cooking time: 15 minutes
Serves 6

- 80g (2¾oz) cornflour
- 1 litre (1¾ pints) cold milk
- 100g (3½oz) caster sugar
- 1 teaspoon bitter almond essence
- finely grated zest of 1 unwaxed lemon
- ½ vanilla pod
- pinch of ground cinnamon
- 50g (1¾oz) pistachios, roughly chopped
- 50g (1¾oz) toasted almonds, roughly chopped
- 50g (1¾oz) plain dark chocolate, shaved into curls (optional)

In a heavy-based saucepan, mix the cornflour with a little of the cold milk until smooth. Stir in the sugar and gradually add the rest of the milk, a little at a time, the bitter almond essence, lemon zest and ½ vanilla pod. Heat gently, stirring constantly with a whisk, until the mixture thickens.

Pour into individual moulds, cool and then chill in the refrigerator for 6 hours.

To serve, unmould, dust with the cinnamon and top with the pistachios, almonds and chocolate curls (if using).

Tip

In the region of Modica, in the southeast of Sicily, cows' milk is replaced with almond milk to which 50g (1¾oz) of ground almonds is added. This is called *gelo di mandorle*.

Fig biscuits
Cuccidati

It is a tradition that every family bakes *cuccidati* – which are also called *buccellati*, depending on who makes them – at Christmastime. They can be prepared in advance and kept in a pretty tin.

Preparation time: 30 minutes
Chilling time: overnight, plus 30 minutes
Cooking time: 40 minutes
Serves 6–8

For the filling:
- 10g (¼oz) raisins
- 150ml (5fl oz) dry Marsala (or port)
- 250g (9oz) almonds
- 100g (3½oz) walnuts, chopped
- 100g (3½oz) pistachios, chopped
- 4 tablespoons honey
- 4 tablespoons marmalade
- 2 teaspoons ground cinnamon
- 1 teaspoon ground cloves
- 500g (1lb 2oz) dried figs, cut into small pieces
- finely grated zest of 1 orange
- 4–5 teaspoons cocoa powder

For the dough:
- 350g (12oz) butter, diced
- 100ml (3½fl oz) milk
- 1kg (2lb 4oz) type '00' flour, plus extra for dusting
- 2 × sachets (11g/¼oz) baking powder
- 200g (7oz) caster sugar
- 3 eggs, beaten
- grated zest of 1 unwaxed lemon
- 2 egg yolks, beaten
- icing sugar, to decorate

Prepare the filling the day before you cook the biscuits. Soak the raisins in the Marsala for about 10 minutes. Toast the almonds, walnuts and pistachios in a dry frying pan or the oven, then grind them very coarsely.

Add all the nuts to a saucepan with the honey, marmalade, ground cinnamon and cloves, chopped figs, orange zest, cocoa powder and the soaked raisins with the Marsala. Cook over a low heat for about 15 minutes, stirring regularly until the mixture has a paste-like consistency. You can blend it with an immersion blender if you feel the pieces of dried fruit are too big. Cool, then chill in the refrigerator overnight.

To prepare the dough, melt the butter in a small saucepan with the milk then leave to cool.

Sift the flour into a large bowl and stir in the baking powder and sugar. Make a well in the centre and add the 3 beaten eggs, lemon zest, melted butter and milk. Mix all the ingredients together, then knead to make a smooth dough (add a little extra water or milk, if needed). Shape into a ball, wrap in clingfilm and leave to rest in the refrigerator for 30 minutes.

To assemble the biscuits, roll out the dough thinly on a lightly floured work surface to form a strip 10–15cm (4–6in) long, 8–10cm (3¼–4in) wide and 1–2cm (½–¾in) thick. Shape the fig paste into a roll and place down the middle of the pastry strip. Fold the strip over the fig paste roll from one long side to form a roll. Cut the roll at intervals at an angle to make small biscuits. Place them on a baking sheet lined with nonstick baking paper and brush them with the beaten egg yolks.

Preheat the oven to 180°C (350°F), Gas Mark 4. Bake the biscuits for about 20 minutes. Leave them to cool and serve dusted with icing sugar.

Tips

Each family has a different way of presenting these biscuits. If you want yours to be the same as the photograph, form each filled biscuit into a circular hoop, seal the joined ends with a little beaten egg, then make cuts on the surface. Top each one with a halved glacé cherry.

Accompany with a passito di Pantelleria, or one of Sicily's dessert wines.

Arancini with chocolate cream

Arancini con crema fondente

This is a classic dessert from the Palermo region, which is also eaten on Santa Lucia's feast day, 13 December. It is absolutely delicious!

Preparation time: 20 minutes
Resting time: 24 hours
Cooking time: 35 minutes
Makes around 15

For the chocolate cream:
- 200g (7oz) double cream
- 1 teaspoon honey
- 125g (4½oz) plain dark chocolate, 85% cocoa solids, chopped

For the arancini:
- 550ml (19fl oz) milk
- 100g (3½oz) Vialone Nano (or Arborio) rice
- 35g (1¼oz) caster sugar
- small pinch of salt
- 1 vanilla pod
- finely grated zest of 1 unwaxed orange
- 1–2 eggs, beaten
- 150g (5½oz) dry (stale) brioche, grated into breadcrumbs
- oil, for deep-frying
- icing sugar, for dusting

The day before serving, prepare the chocolate cream. Mix the cream and honey together in a saucepan and bring to the boil. Add the chopped chocolate and stir over a low heat until the chocolate has melted. Remove the pan from the heat and stir until smooth. Set aside for 24 hours.

The following day, prepare the arancini. Pour the milk into a saucepan and stir in the rice, sugar, salt, vanilla pod and orange zest. Simmer gently over a low heat for 20–25 minutes, stirring regularly. Remove from the heat and leave to cool, then remove the vanilla pod. Using an ice-cream scoop, shape a ball of rice. Place a small spoonful of the chocolate cream in the centre and tightly enclose it in the ball. Repeat to make about 15 balls.

Put the beaten eggs in a shallow bowl and the brioche breadcrumbs into another. Coat the arancini balls first in beaten egg, then in the crumbs.

Heat enough oil for deep-frying in a deep-sided saucepan to 180–190°C (350–375°F), or until a cube of bread browns in 30 seconds. Fry the arancini, in batches, until golden brown. Drain on nonstick baking paper and serve immediately, dusted with icing sugar.

Tip

After cooking, you can roll the arancini in caster sugar and grated cocoa beans for extra flavour and decoration.

Index

A
almond paste 172
almonds 36, 67, 152, 180, 182, 184
anchovy 14, 22, 30, 44, 46, 58, 100
artichokes, Sicilian Violette 78, 100
aubergines, Sicilian Violette 14, 39, 46, 52

B
basil 144
beef 24, 52, 122
black (Venere) rice 92
bottarga 56, 130
breadcrumbs 20, 122
brioche 188
bucatini 58
busiate 67
butter 164

C
calamari 88, 148
candied fruit 158, 172
canned tomatoes 39, 146, 148
cannelloni 76
capers 16, 39, 130, 132, 152
Carnaroli rice 88, 96, 100
casarecce 62
celery 39, 50, 114, 148
chard 44
cherry tomatoes 32, 130, 152
chickpea flour 29
chilli peppers 67
clams 50, 88
cocoa powder 162
cod 16, 132, 138
cooked ham 76, 126
couscous 102, 106
cream 188
cuttlefish 106

D – F
dark chocolate 172, 188
dried figs 184
eggs 44, 84, 110, 114, 116, 120, 138, 158, 180
fennel 44
fish 102
fusilli 67

G – H
garlic 14
honey 174, 180

L
langoustines 96
leeks 16, 96
lemons 140, 164, 168
linguine 78
lobster 96

M
mackerel 154
milk 182, 184
minced meat 110
mortadella 64, 116, 148
mozzarella 126
mussels 50, 88

O
octopus 50, 92, 146
oranges 146, 154, 168, 172, 174

P
Parma ham rind 120
Parmesan 20
parsley 29, 30
peas 24, 100
pecorino 30, 40, 52, 76, 110
penne 56
pistachios 56, 67, 72, 134, 154, 182, 184
pizza dough 30, 32
pork, 110, 120, 122
potatoes 16, 20, 132, 168
prawns 88, 106
pumpkin 36

R
raisins 132, 134, 148, 184, 186
red onions 32, 46, 56
ricotta 44, 62, 72, 76, 84 158, 162, 164, 172
rigatoni 64
round aubergines 62
round-grain rice 24

S
sardines 58, 144
sausagemeat 64, 114
sea bass 134
sea urchin roe 78
shortcrust pastry 40
sourdough 14
spaghetti 72
spinach 84, 148
swordfish 152

T – V
tomato purée 24, 46, 52
tomatoes 30, 67, 96, 102, 140, 144
tuna 32, 140
turbot 130
veal 64, 114, 116, 126
Vialone Nano rice 188

Acknowledgements

I want to thank my family for instilling in me a taste and passion for good food, especially my mother, who introduced me to Sicilian cuisine. It was one that I learnt by watching her and I remember the black cast-iron casserole (which, sixty years later, I still use), in which a *stufato* would be simmering away for hours, to be served with the hundreds of ravioli she had been preparing since early morning. She can be proud of having passed on to me her love of cooking. It is a passion that inspires me and that has naturally led to me writing this book.

I would like to thank my husband Gérard, who has not only helped me in my career but also encouraged me to write the book.

My thanks also go to my sons Alexandre and Stéphane, my favourite recipe testers, for always giving me their opinion when it came to selecting products for the shop, but also – and most importantly – for appreciating their mother's cooking.

My thanks go to my friend Nadine Venier for her valuable assistance and for the good times we've shared.

I'd also like to thank Gaëlle Galindo, who helped me with this project, because I have to confess that I feel more at home in front of a stove than in front of a computer! Thank you to Aurélie Cazenave, my editor and 'fairy godmother', for her faith in me. I salute her professionalism and kindness. My thanks go also to the talented Sandra Mahut, whose photographs of my dishes and the Sicilian landscapes have brought this 'recipe book' to life and hopefully will inspire you to want to cook and travel.

And, finally, here is my recipe for good food. Mix together the following ingredients:
- Curiosity, to look for and discover good ingredients
- Desire, to learn how to cook so you can eat well
- Love, to share with your family and friends
- Passion, since, as with everything you do, if you're passionate about something, everything is made easier
- Time, because taking the time to cook gives pleasure to others.

I invite you to try my recipes, as they are simple, accessible, delicious and – most important – tried and tested!

So now it's over to you...

Enza

I would like to thank Aurélie Cazenave and Chloé Eve for their support throughout this project, which has been so rich in images and emotions. I'd also like to thank André from Le Bontà di Gioia *épicerie* in Paris for his help and his passion for Sicilian cuisines, plus Ronan and Hanawa (and not forgetting Nana, the dog) from the hotel Lùme on the island of Ortigia for the useful addresses they passed on. My thanks also go to Grazia for supplying the fresh pasta and to my mother for all her help. Last, but certainly not least, Enza Genovese for having written such good recipes. It was a pleasure to photograph them.

Sandra

UK/US terms

INGREDIENTS

aubergine – eggplant
bicarbonate of soda – baking soda
broad beans – fava beans
caster sugar – superfine sugar
chickpea flour – gram flour or besan
chickpeas – garbanzo beans
coriander – cilantro
cornflour – cornstarch
courgette – zucchini
crayfish – crawfish
double cream – heavy cream
golden syrup – substitute corn syrup
icing sugar – confectioners' sugar
king prawns – jumbo shrimp
minced beef/lamb/pork/veal – ground beef/lamb/pork/veal
pepper (red/green/yellow) – bell pepper
pine nuts – pine kernels
plain flour – all-purpose flour
rocket – arugula
stock – broth
tomato purée – tomato paste

EQUIPMENT

baking paper – parchment paper
baking tin – baking pan
cake tin – cake pan
clingfilm – plastic wrap
frying pan – skillet
grill – broiler
kitchen paper – paper towels
muffin tin – muffin pan
roasting tray – roasting pan
sieve – fine-mesh strainer
tea towel – dish towel
work surface – countertop

First published in Great Britain in 2025 by Mitchell Beazley, an imprint of Octopus Publishing Group Ltd, Carmelite House. 50 Victoria Embankment, London EC4Y 0DZ
www.octopusbooks.co.uk
www.octopusbooksusa.com

An Hachette UK Company
www.hachette.co.uk

The authorized representative in the EEA is Hachette Ireland, 8 Castlecourt Centre, Dublin 15, D15 XTP3, Ireland (email: info@hbgi.ie)

Originally published in France as *Sicile: Recettes familiales et souvenirs* by Éditions Mango in 2024.

Copyright for original French edition © Mango 2024

Copyright for English © Octopus Publishing Group Ltd 2025

Distributed in the US by Hachette Book Group, 1290 Avenue of the Americas, 4th and 5th Floors, New York, NY 10104

Distributed in Canada by Canadian Manda Group, 664 Annette St., Toronto, Ontario, Canada M6S 2C8

All rights reserved. No part of this work may be reproduced or utilized in any form or by any means, electronic or mechanical, including photocopying, recording or by any information storage and retrieval system, without the prior written permission of the publisher.

Enza Genovese asserts the moral right to be identified as the author of this work.

ISBN 978-1-84091-952-3

A CIP catalogue record for this book is available from the British Library.

Printed and bound in China.

10 9 8 7 6 5 4 3 2 1

English edition 2025
Commissioning Editor: Jeannie Stanley
Creative Director: Jonathan Christie
Senior Editor: Leanne Bryan
Translation from the French: JMS Books LLP, Wendy Sweetser
Designer: Jeremy Tilston
Production Controllers: Lucy Carter and Nic Jones

Picture credits
All photographs by Sandra Mahut, except pages 6–7, 9, 12, 34, 42, 49, 54, 60, 68, 82, 86, 108, 128, 143, 150–151, 156, 167, 184 © iStock and © Shutterstock

Styling: Sandra Mahut